BE HEROIC

Be Heroic

WARREN W. WIERSBE

While this book is intended for the reader's personal enjoyment and profit, it is also designed for group study. Study questions are located at the end of the text.

ChariotVICTOR
PUBLISHING
A DIVISION OF COOK COMMUNICATIONS

Victor Books is an imprint of ChariotVictor Publishing,
a division of Cook Communications, Colorado Springs, Colorado 80918.
Cook Communications, Paris, Ontario
Kingsway Communications, Eastbourne, England

Editor: Barbara Williams
Design: Bill Gray
Cover Photo: FPG International
Study Questions: Susan Moroney

1 2 3 4 5 6 7 8 9 10 Printing / Year 01 00 99 98 97

CONTENTS

PREFACE

Will Rogers once said, "We can't all be heroes, because somebody has to sit on the curb and clap as they go by."

But we can all be heroes, at least from God's point of view; and that's far more important than the applause of the crowd on the curb. Those 50,000 Jewish exiles who returned to Jerusalem to rebuild their temple and their lives were certainly heroes, the kind of heroes whose courage and sacrifice God's people would do well to imitate today.

Their story is told in the Old Testament Books of Ezra, Nehemiah, Haggai, and Zechariah.[1] Ezra was a priest and Haggai and Zechariah were prophets, but together with Zerubbabel the governor of Judah, they encouraged the Jewish remnant, overcame obstacles, and worked together to finish the work God gave them to do. That's what makes heroes.

"Most people aren't appreciated enough," wrote Peggy Noonan in *What I Saw at the Revolution*, "and the bravest things we do in our lives are known only to ourselves. No one throws ticker tape on the man who chose to be faithful to his wife, on the lawyer who didn't take the drug money, or the daughter who held her tongue again and again. All this is anonymous heroism."

God is challenging us to be heroic in a world that desperately needs everyday anonymous heroes who will sacrifice and serve only to hear their Master say, "Well done!"

Will you be among them?

Warren W. Wiersbe

A TIME-LINE

605	First Jewish exiles deported to Babylon
597	Second deportation to Babylon
586	Jerusalem destroyed by Nebuchadnezzar—Third deportation to Babylon
539	Cyrus, King of Persia, conquers Babylon
538	Cyrus issues his decree to the Jewish exiles
537	About 50,000 Jews return to the land, led by Zerubbabel and Joshua
536	Foundation of the temple laid
536–520	Work interrupted because of official opposition
520	Work resumed; ministry of Haggai and Zechariah
515	The temple completed
458	Ezra the scribe arrives in Jerusalem
444	Nehemiah arrives; walls rebuilt, gates restored

A Suggested Outline of the Book of Ezra

Key theme: Restoring the spiritual heart of the nation
Key verse: Ezra 7:10

I. The nation is restored—1–6
   1. A remnant returns with Zerubbabel and Joshua—1–2
   2. The temple is rebuilt—3–6
      (1) The work begins—3
      (2) The work opposed—4
      (3) The work resumed—5
      (4) The work completed—6

II. The people are rededicated—7–10
   1. A second group arrives with Ezra—7–8
   2. Confession of sin—9
   3. Cleansing of sin—10

The Providence of God

"Thank God He gives us difficult things to do!" said Oswald Chambers in *My Utmost for His Highest.*[1]

The first time I read that statement, I shook my head in disagreement; but I was young and inexperienced then, and it seemed smarter to do the easy things that made me look successful. However, I've lived long enough to understand the wisdom of Chambers' statement. I've learned that when God tells us to do difficult things, it's because He wants us to grow. Unlike modern-day press agents and spin doctors, God doesn't manufacture synthetic heroes; He grows the real thing. "The hero was a big man," wrote Daniel Boorstin; "the celebrity is a big name."[2]

In God's Hall of Heroes are the names of nearly 50,000 Jews who in 538 B.C. left captivity in Babylon for responsibility in Jerusalem. God had called them back home to do a difficult job: to rebuild the temple and the city and restore the Jewish community in their own land. This noble venture involved a four months' journey plus a great deal of faith, courage, and sacrifice; and even after they arrived in the Holy City, life didn't get any easier. But as you read the inspired record, you can see the providential leading of the

Lord from start to finish; and "if God be for us, who can be against us?" (Rom. 8:31)

You see God's providence at work in three key events.

1. The release of the captives (Ezra 1:1-4)

More than a century before, the Prophet Isaiah had warned the Jews that the people of Judah would be taken captive by Babylon and punished for their sins (Isa. 6:11-12; 11:11-12; 39:5-7), and his prophecy was fulfilled. In 605, Nebuchadnezzar deported the royal family and took the temple vessels to Babylon. In 597, he sent into exile 7,000 "men of might" and a thousand craftsmen (2 Kings 24:10-16); and in 586, he destroyed Jerusalem and the temple and exiled the rest of the Jews in Babylon, except for "the poor of the land" (2 Kings 25:1-21).

In 538, Cyrus the Great, king of Persia, conqueror of Babylon, issued a decree that permitted the exiled Jews to return to their land and rebuild their temple. This too had been prophesied by Isaiah (Isa. 44:28). What Cyrus did twenty-five centuries ago reminds us today of some important spiritual truths.

God is faithful to His Word. For at least forty years, the Prophet Jeremiah had warned the leaders of Judah that the Babylonian exile was inevitable (see Jer. 20:4-6; 21:7-10); and he pled with them to repent of their sins and surrender to Babylon. Only then could they save the city and the temple from ruin. The leaders didn't listen—in fact, they called Jeremiah a traitor—and the Holy City and the temple were destroyed in 587–586.

But Jeremiah also announced that the Captivity would be for seventy years (Jer. 25:1-14; 29:10; see Dan. 9:1-2). Bible students don't agree on the dating of this period, whether it begins with the Babylonian invasion in 606 or the destruction of the city and temple in 587–586. From

606 to 537–536, when the remnant returned to Judah, is seventy years; but so also is the period from the fall of Jerusalem (586) to the completion of the second temple in 516. Regardless of which calculation you accept, the prediction and its fulfillment are astonishing.[3] Whether He promises chastening or blessing, God is always faithful to His Word. "Not one thing has failed of all the good things which the Lord your God spoke concerning you" (Josh. 23:14, NKJV). "There has not failed one word of all His good promise" (1 Kings 8:56, NKJV). "Heaven and earth shall pass away," said Jesus, "but My words shall not pass away" (Matt. 24:35).

God is faithful to His covenant. In spite of their sins, these exiles were God's chosen people and children of the covenant He had made with Abraham, Isaac, and Jacob (Gen. 12:1-3). The nation had broken the covenant, but the Lord had remained faithful to His Word. He had called the Jewish nation to bring blessing to all the earth, and He would see to it that they fulfilled their mission. Through them, the world would receive the knowledge of the one true and living God, the written Word of God, and ultimately the Savior of the world. "Salvation is of the Jews" (John 4:22).

God is in control of the nations. It was the Lord who raised up Nebuchadnezzar—"My servant" (Jer. 25:9; 27:6; 43:10)—to chasten the people of Judah; and then He raised up Cyrus to defeat the Babylonians and establish the Persian Empire. "Who has stirred up one from the east, calling him in righteousness to His service? He hands nations over to him and subdues kings before him" (Isa. 41:2, NIV; see also v. 25). The Lord called Cyrus "My shepherd" (44:28) and "His anointed" (45:1), and Isaiah prophesied that Cyrus would liberate the exiles and enable them to rebuild their city and temple (v. 13).

God's people need to remember that the Lord God is sovereign over all nations and can do what He pleases with the most powerful rulers. Nebuchadnezzar had to learn this lesson the hard way (Dan. 4:28-32), but then he confessed: "His [God's] dominion is an everlasting dominion, and His kingdom is from generation to generation. All the inhabitants of the earth are reputed as nothing; He does according to His will in the army of heaven and among the inhabitants of the earth. No one can restrain His hand" (Dan. 4:34-35).

God can do as He pleases with the rulers of the earth; and He has demonstrated this in His dealings with Pharaoh (Ex. 9:16; Rom. 9:17), Ahasuerus (The Book of Esther), Sennacherib (2 Kings 19:28), Augustus Caesar (Luke 2:1), and Herod Agrippa I (Acts 12:20-24). King Jehoshaphat said it perfectly: "O Lord, God of our fathers, are You not the God who is in heaven? You rule over all the kingdoms of the nations. Power and might are in Your hand, and no one can withstand You" (2 Chron. 20:6).

People don't have to be Christian believers for God to use them. Whether a mayor, governor, senator, prime minister, ambassador, or president, God can exercise His sovereign power to accomplish His purposes for His people. This is one reason Paul exhorts believers to pray for those in authority, not that our political agenda might be fulfilled, but that God's will might be accomplished on this earth (1 Tim. 2:1-8). "God can make a straight stroke with a crooked stick," said Puritan preacher John Watson; and that's what he did with Cyrus!

The king's decree boldly acknowledged the Lord and called Him "the Lord God of heaven" (Ezra 1:2), a title that's used seventeen times in Ezra, Nehemiah, and Daniel. The decree addressed two kinds of people: (1) those who wanted to return to their land and (2) those who preferred to remain in Babylon. The latter group was urged to give offerings to help finance the expenses of the journey and the restoration of the temple.[4]

The Jews also accepted gifts from their Gentile neighbors (v. 6, NIV). When the Jews left Egypt, they plundered the Egyptians (Ex. 12:35-36) and collected the wages the men should have received during their years of slavery. Now the Jews were making their "exodus" from captivity, so they collected wealth from their pagan neighbors and dedicated it to the Lord [5]

2. The return of the remnant (Ezra 1:5–2:70)
God not only stirred the spirit of Cyrus to grant freedom to the captives (1:1), but He also stirred the hearts of the Jews to give them the desire to return to Judah (v. 5). "For it is God who works in you both to will and to do for His good pleasure" (Phil. 2:13). The same God who ordains the end (the rebuilding of the temple) also ordains the means to the end, in this case, a people willing to go to Judah and work.

The treasure (Ezra 1:5-11). Not only did the travelers carry their own personal belongings, but they carried 5,400 gold and silver temple vessels which had been taken from Jerusalem by Nebuchadnezzar (2 Kings 25:8-17; Jer. 52:17-23; Dan. 1:2; 5:1-3).These items were carefully inventoried by the treasurer and delivered to Sheshbazzar, the appointed ruler of Judah.

Who was Sheshbazzar? He's mentioned four times in Ezra (1:8, 11; 5:14, 16) but not once in any of the other post-exilic books. He's called "the prince of Judah" (1:8, KJV, NIV), a title that can mean "leader" or "captain" and often referred to the heads of the tribes of Israel (Num. 1:16, 44; 7:2; Josh. 9:15-21). The word "Judah" in Ezra 1:8 refers to the district of Judah in the Persian Empire, not to the tribe of Judah; so Sheshbazzar was the appointed leader of "the children of the province [of Judah]" (Ezra 2:1).

Many Bible students believe that Sheshbazzar was another name for Zerubbabel, the governor of Judah, who with Joshua the high priest directed the work of the remnant as they rebuilt the city and the temple. He's mentioned twenty times in the postexilic books, and according to 2 Chronicles 3:16-19 was a grandson of King Jehoiakim and therefore a descendant of David.

Ezra 5:16 states that Sheshbazzar laid the foundation of the temple, while Ezra 3:8-13 attributes this to Zerubbabel, and Zechariah 4:9 confirms it. It seems logical to conclude that Sheshbazzar and Zerubbabel were the same person. It wasn't unusual in that day for people to have more than one given name, especially if you were a Jew born in a foreign land.

When you add the numbers given in Ezra 1:9-10, they total 2,499; but the total given in verse 11 is 5,400. A contradiction? Not necessarily, for it was important that Zerubbabel and the leaders keep a careful inventory of the temple treasure, and it's not likely they would make that big a blunder. The statement in 1:10, "and other vessels a thousand" suggests that verses 9-10 list the larger and more valuable items, while many smaller objects weren't even listed in categories.

The leaders (2:1-2). From the parallel list in Nehemiah 7, we must add the name of Nahamani (Ezra 2:7), bringing the total to twelve men, one for each of the tribes. The Nehemiah in verse 2 is not the man who rebuilt the walls of Jerusalem, because he didn't come on the scene until 444. And the Mordecai listed isn't the Mordecai of the Book of Esther. "Jeshua" is Joshua the high priest, who is mentioned twenty-three times in the postexilic writings. He was an important part of the leadership of the remnant and served at the side of Zerubbabel the governor.

Geographically, the Southern Kingdom (Judah) included

only the tribes of Judah and Benjamin; but over the years, people from the other ten tribes had moved to Judah, so that all twelve tribes were represented in the Captivity. The Bible says nothing about "ten lost tribes"; it appears that all twelve are accounted for (James 1:1; Acts 26:7).

Everything in God's work rises and falls with leadership. When God wants to accomplish something, He calls dedicated men and women to challenge His people and lead the way. A decay in the quality of a nation's leaders is an indication that trouble is ahead. The British essayist Walter Savage Landor wrote, "When small men cast long shadows, it's a sign that the sun is setting."

The families and clans (Ezra 1:3-35). The long lists of names given in Scripture, including the genealogies, may not be interesting to the average reader, but they're very important to the history of God's people. Unless there's an inheritance involved, most people today are more concerned about the behavior of their descendants than the bloodline of their ancestors; but that wasn't true of the Old Testament Jews. It was necessary for them to be able to prove their ancestry for many reasons.

To begin with, unless you could prove your ancestry, you couldn't enter into the rights and privileges of the Jewish nation, of which there were many. The Israelites were a covenant people with an important God-given task to fulfill on earth, and they couldn't allow outsiders to corrupt them. Furthermore, the Jews returning to Judah couldn't reclaim their family property unless they could prove their lineage. Of course, it was especially important that the priests and Levites certify their ancestry; otherwise they couldn't serve in the temple or share in the benefits of that service, such as the tithes and offerings and the assigned portions of the sacrifices.

In verses 3-20, the names of eighteen Jewish families are

listed, totaling 15,604 males. When they took a census, the Jews usually included men twenty years of age and older (Num. 1:1-4); but we aren't certain what procedure was followed here. In Ezra 1:21-35, the volunteers were listed according to twenty-one cities and villages, a total of 8,540 men. We don't know the names of all these 24,144 men, but they were important to the Lord and to the future of the nation and its ministry to the world.

The priests and Levites were especially important to the nation (vv. 36-42), for without them, there would be no reason to rebuild the temple. Four groups of priests totaled 4,289 men, and they would be assisted by 341 Levites, some of whom were singers and gatekeepers. The Levites also assisted the priests in teaching the people the law of the Lord (Deut. 33:8-10; Neh. 8:5-8).

The 392 "Nethinim" (Ezra 1:43-54) and "children of Solomon's servants" (vv. 55-58) were workers in the temple who were not priests or Levites. In Hebrew, "Nethinim" means "those given" and seems to refer to prisoners of war who were given to the priests to perform menial tasks in the temple. (See Josh. 9:23, 27 and Num. 31:30, 47.) "Solomon's servants" were probably a similar group of men, established during Solomon's reign. Eighty years later, Ezra would have to send for more Levites and Nethinim to help with the temple ministry (Ezra 8:15-20).

The disqualified (Ezra 1:59-63). There were 652 people who couldn't prove their Jewish ancestry. (The towns mentioned were in Babylon, not Judah.) Zerubbabel and Joshua didn't send these people back home but allowed them the rights of "strangers and foreigners" (Ex. 22:21, 24; 23:9; Lev. 19:33-34; Deut. 10:18; 14:29).

We aren't told how many priests were unable to provide adequate credentials, but we are told that they were excluded from serving in the temple. No doubt some men thought they could enter the priesthood and have a much easier time living in Jerusalem, but Zerubbabel rejected them. God had made it clear that any outsider who attempted to serve at the altar would be put to death (Num. 1:51; 3:10). These men were treated as "strangers" and allowed to make the journey, but Zerubbabel the governor[6] excluded them from the priestly privileges until they could be tested by "the Urim and Thummim."[7] This was the means provided for the high priest to determine God's will (Ex. 28:30; Num. 27:21).

The totals (Ezra 1:64-67). The total that Ezra gives (42,360) is 12,542 more than the total you get when you add up the individual figures given in the chapter. Nehemiah also gives 42,360 (Neh. 7:66). However, in giving this list, Ezra didn't say that these several groups represented all the men who left Babylon, nor do we know how many more joined after the list was completed. It's possible that he counted men only from Judah and Benjamin, so that pilgrims from the other ten tribes make up the difference.

We do know that an additional 7,337 servants, both men and women, went along, which speaks well of their Jewish masters and mistresses, for these servants (slaves?) might have been sold in Babylon and remained there. Apparently, they preferred to be with the Jews. This many servants (one-sixth of the total) also suggests that some of the Jews had become wealthy in Babylon.

The 200 singers (Ezra 1:65) were not a part of the temple ministry but were "secular singers" who performed for Jewish festive occasions such as weddings (see 2 Chron. 35:25). From the time of the Exodus (Ex. 15), the Jews composed songs to honor God and celebrate the blessings of life. Over a dozen different musical instruments are named in Scripture. The captivity in Babylon hadn't been a time for singing (Ps. 137:1-4); but now that the Jews were "heading home," they had a song to sing.

3. The rebuilding of the temple (Ezra 2:68–3:13)

Ezra wrote nothing about the long trip (900 miles) or what the Jews experienced during those four difficult months. It reminds us of Moses' description of Abraham and Sarah's journey to Canaan: "and they went forth to go into the land of Canaan; and into the land of Canaan they came" (Gen. 12:5). "It is a strange narrative of a journey," said Alexander Maclaren, "which omits the journey altogether . . . and notes but its beginning and its end. Are these not the main points in every life, its direction and its attainment?" [8]

Investing in the work (Ezra 2:68-70). This was undoubtedly a thank offering to the Lord for giving them a safe journey. The people gave their offerings willingly and according to their ability, which is the way God's people are supposed to give today (2 Cor. 8:8-15; 9:6-15). According to Nehemiah 7:70-72, both the tribal leaders and Zerubbabel the governor gave generously, and the common people followed their good example.

Setting up the altar (Ezra 3:1-3). The seventh month would be Tishri, our September–October, a month very sacred to the Jews (Lev. 23:23-44). It opened with the Feast of Trumpets; the Day of Atonement was on the tenth day; and from the fifteenth to the twenty-first days, they celebrated the Feast of Tabernacles. But the first thing Joshua the high priest did was restore the altar so he could offer sacrifices for the people. The people were afraid of the strong nations around them who resented the return of the Jews, and they wanted to be sure they were pleasing to the Lord. Again, we see a parallel with Abraham, who built an altar when he first came into the land of Canaan (Gen. 12:7). This is an Old Testament picture of Matthew 6:33.

Joshua also restored the various sacrifices commanded by the Law, which would include a burnt offering each morning and evening and extra offerings for special days. It wasn't necessary to wait until the temple was completed before offering sacrifices to God. As long as there was a sanctified altar and a qualified priest, sacrifices could be given to the Lord. After all, it's not the external furnishings but what's in the heart that concerns God the most (1 Sam. 15:22; Ps. 51:16-17; Hosea 6:6; Mark 12:28-34).

Laying the foundation (Ezra 3:7-13). The work didn't begin until the second month of the next year, which means they spent nearly seven months gathering materials and preparing to build. It was in the second month that Solomon started building the original temple (1 Kings 6:1), and he gathered his materials in much the same way (Ezra 3:7; 1 Kings 5:6-12). Joshua and Zerubbabel were in charge of the project, assisted by the Levites. "If the foundations are destroyed, what can the righteous do?" asked David (Ps. 11:3); and there's only one answer: lay the foundations again! That's what spiritual revival is all about, getting back to the foundations of the Christian life and making sure they're solid: repentance, confession, prayer, the Word of God, obedience, and faith.

Note the emphasis on unity. The people gathered together (Ezra 3:1); the workers stood together (v. 9); the Levites sang together (v. 11); and all the while, the people were working together to get the foundation laid. Their tasks were varied, but they all had one goal before them: to glorify the Lord by rebuilding His temple. This is what Paul had in mind when he wrote "make my joy complete by being like-minded, having the same love, being one in spirit and purpose" (Phil. 2:2).

Following the example of David, when he brought up the ark to Jerusalem (1 Chron. 16), and Solomon, when he dedicated the temple (2 Chron. 7:1-3), the priests and Levites sang praise to the Lord, accompanied by trumpets and cymbals; and the people responded with a great shout that was heard afar off. (See Pss. 47:1; 106:1; 107:1; 118:1-4; 135:3; 136; and 145:1-11.) The people united their hearts and voices in praise to the Lord for His goodness to them.

But at this point, their "togetherness" was interrupted as the young men shouted for joy and the old men wept "with a loud voice." Why were they weeping on such a joyful occasion? Because they had seen the original temple before it was destroyed over fifty years before, and the new edifice was nothing in comparison. (Haggai would later preach a sermon about this. See Hag. 2:1-9.) These godly old men longed for "the good old days," but it was the sins of their generation that had caused the fall of the kingdom to begin with! Had their generation listened to the Prophet Jeremiah and obeyed God's Word, Jerusalem and the temple would still be standing.

It's unfortunate when the unity of God's people is shattered because generations look in opposite directions. The older men were looking back with longing while the younger men were looking around with joy. Both of them should have been looking up and praising the Lord for what He had accomplished. We certainly can't ignore the past, but the past must be a rudder to guide us and not an anchor to hold us back. God's people are a family, not a family album filled with old pictures; they're a garden, not a graveyard covered with monuments to past successes.

We have similar generational disagreements in the church today, especially when it comes to styles of worship. Older saints enjoy singing the traditional hymns with their doctrinal substance, but younger members of the church want worship that has a more contemporary approach. But it isn't a question of accepting the one and rejecting the other, unless you want to divide families and split the church. It's a matter of balance: the old must learn from the young and the young from the old, in a spirit of love and submission (1 Peter

5:1-11). When they were new, many of our traditional hymns were rejected for the same reasons some people reject contemporary praise choruses today. "But each class [the young and the old] should try to understand the other's feelings," said Alexander Maclaren. "The seniors think the juniors revolutionary and irreverent; the juniors think the seniors fossils. It is possible to unite the shout of joy and the weeping. Unless a spirit of reverent regard for the past presides over the progressive movements of this or any day, they will not lay a solid foundation for the temple of the future. We want the old and the young to work side by side, if the work is to last and the sanctuary is to be ample enough to embrace all shades of character and tendencies of thought."[9]

Every local church is but one generation short of extinction. If the older believers don't challenge and equip the younger Christians and set a godly example before them (Titus 2:1-8; 1 Tim. 5:1-2), the future of the congregation is in jeopardy. The church is a family; and as a family grows and matures, some things have to fall away and other things take their place. This happens in our homes and it must happen in the house of God. To some people, "change" is a synonym for "compromise," but where there's love, "change" becomes a synonym for "cooperation with one another and concern for one another."

"Behold, how good and how pleasant it is for brethren to dwell together in unity!" (Ps. 133:1)

T W O

The Faithfulness of God

"Therefore know that the Lord your God, He is God, the faithful God" (Deut. 7:9, NKJV). Moses said that to the new generation of Israelites before they entered Canaan, a truth they would need as they faced the enemy and claimed their inheritance. New generations and old generations both need to be reminded that God is faithful.

"He who calls you is faithful, who also will do it" (1 Thes. 5:24, NKJV). Paul wrote that to some young Christians in Thessalonica, people who were being persecuted for their faith. They needed to be reminded that God's commandments are God's enablements.

"God being who He is," said A.W. Tozer, "cannot cease to be what He is, and being what He is, He cannot act out of character with Himself. He is at once faithful and immutable, so all His words and acts must be and must remain faithful."[1]

J. Hudson Taylor, pioneer missionary to inland China, described the successful Christian life as "not a striving to have faith . . . but a looking off to the Faithful One . . . "[2] He knew the words of Paul: "If we are faithless, He remains faithful. He cannot deny Himself" (2 Tim. 2:13, NKJV).

The Jewish remnant that returned to Jerusalem to rebuild

the temple was depending on God's faithfulness to see them through. If God wasn't faithful to His covenant and His promises, then there was no hope. But the God who called them would be faithful to help them finish His work (Phil. 1:6), as long as they trusted Him and obeyed His Word.

In these three chapters, we see how God was faithful to His people in every stage of their work for Him.

1. Stage one: the work opposed (Ezra 4:1-24)

From the beginning, the remnant faced opposition from the mixed population of the land who really didn't want the Jews inhabiting Jerusalem and rebuilding the temple. Opportunity and opposition usually go together; and the greater the opportunity, the greater the opposition. "For a great and effective door has opened to me," wrote Paul, "and there are many adversaries" (1 Cor. 16:9).

Cooperation leading to compromise (Ezra 4:1-3). The first attack of the enemy was very subtle: the people of Samaria, the former Northern Kingdom, offered to work with the Jews to help them build the temple. These people claimed to worship the same God the Jews worshiped, so it seemed logical that they should be allowed to share in the work. On the surface, the Samaritans seemed to be acting like good neighbors, but their offer was insidious and dangerous.

The Samaritan people, being a mixture of many races, weren't true Jews at all. When the Assyrians conquered the Northern Kingdom, they deliberately mingled the nations they had defeated; and this led to racial and religious confusion (2 Kings 17:24-41). The Samaritans didn't worship the true and living God, for they "feared the Lord, yet served their own gods" (2 Kings 17:33; see John 4:22). The Jewish leaders had already rejected the professed Jews who had been in exile in Babylon (Ezra 2:59-63), so they weren't about to accept the people of the land who obviously didn't belong to the covenant nation and couldn't prove their Jewish lineage.

Why was the Samaritan offer so dangerous? Because if these outsiders had begun to mingle with the Jewish remnant while helping to build the temple, it wouldn't have taken long for the two groups to start socializing and intermarrying; and that was contrary to the Law of Moses (Ex. 34:10-17; Deut. 7:1-11; 12:1-3). Israel was a nation set apart from the other nations (Num. 23:9), because God had given them a special task to perform in the world (Gen. 12:1-3). If in any way the people of Israel were corrupted, the success of their God-given ministry would be jeopardized.

God's people today must maintain a separated position and not get involved with anything that will compromise their testimony and hinder God's work (2 Cor. 6:14–7:1; 2 Tim. 2:3-5).

However, separation must never become isolation (1 Cor. 5:9-10) because God has a work for believers to do in this world (Matt. 5:13-16; John 17:14-18). Jesus was "holy, harmless, undefiled, separate from sinners" (Heb. 7:26); and yet He was the friend of sinners and sought to win them (Luke 15:1-2; Matt. 9:10-11; 11:19). God's people separate from the world so they can be a witness to the world.

Accusation leading to fear (Ezra 4:4-5, 24). Satan had come as the serpent to deceive (2 Cor. 11:3) and had failed; and now he came as the lion to devour (1 Peter 5:8), and he succeeded. The enemy told lies about the Jews and encouraged the people of the land to do everything possible to discourage the workers and hinder the work. They even hired counselors to influence the local officials to stop the project, and they succeeded.

"Then ceased the work of the house of God which is at Jerusalem" (Ezra 4:24). This was during the reign of Cyrus (559–530) who had given the Jews the right to return to their land and rebuild their temple. From 536 to 530, the work had progressed; but in 530, it stopped and didn't resume until the year 520, when Darius was king. This defeat wasn't because the king had issued a decree against them, but because the Jewish remnant feared the people of the land. The Jews had begun to get more interested in their own houses than in the house of God (Hag. 1:1-11).

Other opposition to God's work (Ezra 4:6-23). At this point in the narrative (vv. 6-23), Ezra cited other instances of the work being attacked, including the events that occurred during the time of Darius, who reigned from 522 to 486 (vv. 5, 24); Xerxes (v. 6) who was the Ahasuerus of the Book of Esther and reigned from 486 to 465; and Artaxerxes I (vv. 7-23), ruler from 465 to 424. Ancient writers often summarized historical events in this manner before moving on to finish their account. Ezra's main interest, of course, was in the opposition that came while the temple was being rebuilt during the reigns of Cyrus and Darius. The long parenthesis in vv. 6-23 deals with the rebuilding of the city (v. 12) and not the rebuilding of the temple. It's additional evidence of the fact that whenever God's people try to serve the Lord, somebody will oppose them. [3]

In the seventh year of Artaxerxes I (458–457), Ezra the scribe took a group of liberated Jewish exiles to Jerusalem to start rebuilding the city (7:1). Eastern rulers depended on their local officials to act as spies and report anything suspicious. Rehum, the officer in charge, conferred with the other officials and decided that the rebuilding of the city was a threat to the peace of the empire. So he dictated a letter to Shimshai the scribe and had it sent to the king.

Rehum gave four reasons why the king must order the Jews to stop rebuilding Jerusalem. First, history showed that Jerusalem was indeed a "rebellious and wicked city"; unfortunately, this was a fact that even the Jews couldn't deny. If

Jerusalem were restored, Rehum argued, it would rebel against the king and declare its independence (4:12).[4] As long as Jerusalem was in ruins, it was defenseless against the king's forces.

Second, an independent Judah would mean loss of revenue and tribute to the empire (v. 13);[5] but, third, a successful rebellion would also bring dishonor to the king. What king wants to have one of his provinces successfully rebel against him? This might encourage other provinces to follow their example. Finally, if the Jews succeeded in rebuilding and rebelling, they would no doubt conquer the entire territory across the Euphrates (v. 16); and this would really hurt the king and his empire.

The king's officers searched the archives and found proof that the Jews had indeed been ruled by mighty kings (David, Solomon, Josiah, Hezekiah) and also by rebellious kings, so Rehum's accusations were correct. During the declining years of Judah, their kings had made and broken treaties with Egypt, Assyria, and Babylon and had refused to pay tribute to Assyria and to Babylon. Their own record indicted them.

The king ordered the Jews to stop rebuilding the city. In fact, it's likely that the Persians wrecked the work the Jews had already completed, and the report that Nehemiah received from his brother described what the Persians had done, not what the Babylonians had done (Neh. 1:1-3). It wasn't until the arrival of Nehemiah in 445 that the work was resumed and the walls were finished and the gates restored.

2. Stage two: the work resumed (Ezra 5:1–6:12)

From 530 to 520, the Jews concentrated on building their own houses, and neglected the house of the Lord. The Lord chastened His people to encourage them to obey His commands (Hag. 1:6), but they refused to listen. What means did

God use to get the work going again?

God used preachers of the Word (Ezra 5:1-2). It was by the Word of the Lord that the world was created (Ps. 33:6-9), and by that same Word the Lord governs His creation and His people (Ps. 33:10-11). Church history shows that when God wants to arouse His people to do His will, He calls people to proclaim the Word of the Lord. The preaching of Martin Luther brought about what we call "the Reformation," a movement that transformed not only Germany but the entire Christian world. The preaching of John Wesley produced a spiritual awakening in Great Britain that swept many into the kingdom of God. Historians tell us that the Weslyan Revival helped to rescue England from the kind of blood bath that France experienced during the French Revolution.

Never underestimate the power of the faithful preaching of God's Word. Charles Spurgeon, the famed British Baptist preacher, said, "I cannot help feeling that the man who preaches the word of God is standing, not on a mere platform, but on a throne."[6]

Haggai began his ministry of the Word on August 29, 520 (Hag. 1:1), and five of his messages are recorded in the book that bears his name. A month or two later, he was joined by a young man named Zechariah, a priest whom God had called to be a prophet (Zech. 1:1). These two men delivered God's Word to the leaders and the remnant, "and they [the Jews] prospered through the prophesying [preaching] of Haggai, the prophet, and Zechariah" (Ezra 6:14).

Any work of God that isn't built on the Word of God will never prosper. Moses' success as the leader of Israel came from his faith in and obedience to God's Word (Deut. 4:10). Joshua's success in conquering the enemy in Canaan was based on his devotion to the Word of God (Josh. 1:8). When we obey God's Word, we can expect "great reward" (Ps. 19:11). If we want to know the power of God, we must also know the Word of God (Matt. 22:29).

God used local officials (Ezra 5:3-17). As governor of the province of Judah, Tattenai (Tatnai) was concerned about what the Jews were doing in Jerusalem, and rightly so. It was his responsibility to protect the interests of King Darius and the welfare of the empire and to see to it that peace and security were maintained. So, when the project was resumed, Tattenai investigated and asked two questions: (1) "Who gave you the authority to do this?" and (2) "What are the names of the men working on the building?"

The Jews didn't look upon the Persian officer as a trouble-maker, but graciously answered his questions. After all, they had nothing to hide, and the eye of the Lord was upon them. God saw to it that the work was allowed to go on while Tattenai contacted the king to find out what to do.

God's people must "walk in wisdom toward those who are outside" (Col. 4:5, NKJV) and "walk honestly toward them that are outside" (1 Thes. 4:12), otherwise we have no effective witness where a witness is greatly needed. "Everyone must submit himself to the governing authorities, for there is no authority except that which God has established" (Rom. 13:1, NIV; and see 1 Peter 2:11-17). When it comes to the believers' relationship to civil authorities, there's no place for arrogance, accusation, or carnal anger masquerading as zeal for the Lord. Even where we disagree with officials, we can do it graciously (Dan. 1; 3; 6; Acts 4:19-20; 5:29; 1 Peter 2:13-25).

One of the things that worried Tattenai was the structure of the temple, with its large stones and timbered walls. It looked more like a fortress than a sanctuary! And the work was progressing so rapidly that he wondered if the Jews were planning to revolt.

The Jews knew their history and told Tattenai how the temple was built (the "great king" being Solomon) and why the temple was destroyed. They related how Nebuchadnezzar exiled the Jews in Babylon and how decades later Cyrus gave them permission to return to their land and rebuild their temple. Cyrus also gave them the temple treasures so that the ministry could be established again according to the Law of Moses. The facts were all there; the king's secretaries could check the archives to see that the Jews were telling the truth.

Careful to "[make] the most of every opportunity" (Eph. 5:15-16), the Jewish workers framed their answers to glorify the Lord. They didn't try to cover up the sins of the nation (Ezra 5:12) and they openly acknowledged that they were "the servants of the God of heaven" (v. 11). Both in their words and their demeanor, they presented a clear witness to this important Persian official, and God used him to certify their right to build and guarantee supplies from the king!

God used Darius the king (6:1-12). The royal secretaries searched the archives and located the scroll Cyrus had left containing the edict that governed the return of the Jews to their land. It authorized the Jews to rebuild their temple and even gave the limits of its dimensions.[7] Cyrus permitted large stones to be used for the walls and promised to pay the costs from the royal treasury. He also ordered the local officials to provide beasts for the daily sacrifices. His motive here may have been mixed, because he wanted the priests to pray for him and his sons, but the people of God are supposed to pray for those who are in authority (1 Tim. 2:1-4).

"Let the work of this house of God alone!" (Ezra 6:7) literally means, "Keep your distance!" Neither the local Persian officials nor the people of the land were to interfere, but rather do everything they could to support the work. The king described the terrible judgments that would come to anybody who didn't obey his edict (vv. 11-12). So, what started out as an investigation ended up as a royal decree that protected the Jews and provided for them!

But suppose the Jewish remnant had been offensive and treated Tattenai and his associates with defiance and disdain? His letter to headquarters might not have been as positive as it was, and this could have changed everything. Peter admonishes us to speak "with gentleness and respect" (1 Peter 3:15, NIV) when unsaved people question us, because this glorifies God and opens new opportunities for witness. God's eye is upon His people as they serve Him, so we need not fear what men can do to us.

3. Stage three: the work completed (Ezra 6:13-22)

On the twelfth day of the last month of 515, the temple was completed, about seventy years from the destruction of the temple by the Babylonians in 586, and about five and a half years after Haggai and Zechariah called the people back to work (5:1). God had been faithful to care for His people. He provided encouragement through the preaching of the prophets and even used the authority and wealth of a pagan king to further the work.

The joy of dedicating (6:13-18). Though there was no ark in the holy of holies, and no glory filled the house, the temple was still dedicated[8] to the Lord because it was His house, built for His glory. Instead of weeping over what they didn't have, the Jews rejoiced over what they did have, and this is always the attitude of faith.

When King Solomon dedicated the temple that he built, he offered so many sacrifices that they couldn't be counted (1 Kings 8:5), plus 142,000 peace offerings which were shared with the people (1 Kings 8:63). The Jewish remnant offered only 712 sacrifices, but the Lord accepted them. Most important, they offered twelve male goats as sin offerings, one for each tribe, because they wanted the Lord to forgive their sins and give them a new beginning.

Joshua the high priest also consecrated the priests and Levites for their ministry in the completed temple. David had organized the priests into twenty-four courses so they could minister more effectively (1 Chron. 24:1-19). It wasn't necessary for all of them to serve all the time, for each course was assigned its week of ministry at the temple (Luke 1:5, 8). The statement "as it is written in the law of Moses" (6:18) refers to the consecration of the priests, not their organization. (See Lev. 8–9.)

The joy of remembering (Ezra 6:19-22). Passover was just a few weeks later and the Jews gathered in their families to remember how God had delivered them from bondage in Egypt (Ex. 12). Each year, the Jewish men were required to make three trips to Jerusalem to celebrate Passover, Pentecost, and the Feast of Tabernacles. During their years in exile, how the hearts of the Jews must have yearned for the day when once again they were free to go to their Holy City and worship God.

The leaders invited all the Jews and Jewish proselytes to share in the Passover, even those who couldn't prove their lineage. As long as the males were circumcised (Ex. 12:43-49) and had separated themselves from the paganism of the people of the land, they were welcome. It speaks well of the Jewish remnant that they reached out in this way and didn't try to establish an exclusive "holier than thou" fellowship.

The temple had been dedicated, and now the people were dedicating themselves to the Lord. During the seven days of the Feast of Unleavened Bread, the Jews had to remove all yeast (leaven) from their dwellings, a picture of personal purification. To a Jew, yeast was a symbol of evil; so Passover was a time to put away all evil from their lives. What good is a dedicated temple if you don't have a dedicated people? Once again, Jewish worship would take place in the Holy City in a restored temple dedicated to the Lord. No wonder the people were rejoicing! And it was all because of the faithfulness of God. He had "turned the heart of the king"[9] to assist the people, and now the work was completed (Prov. 21:1).

No matter what our circumstances may be, we can trust God to be faithful. "Great is Thy faithfulness" isn't just a verse to quote (Lam. 3:23) or a song to sing. It's a glorious truth to believe and to act upon, no matter how difficult the situation in life might be.

"I will sing of the mercies of the Lord forever; with my mouth I will make known Your faithfulness to all generations" (Ps. 89:1, NKJV).

THREE

The Good Hand of God

When talk show hosts and hostesses ask successful people the "secret" of their great achievements, the answers they get are varied and sometimes contradictory. Some successful people will give credit to their sobriety and personal discipline, while others will boast that they lived just the way they pleased whether anybody liked it or not. "I always maintain my integrity" is counterbalanced by "I pushed my way to the top no matter who got stepped on."

But if we had interviewed Ezra and asked him the secret of his successful life, he would have said humbly, "The good hand of the Lord was upon me,"[1] a phrase that's found six times in Ezra 7 and 8 (7:6, 9, 28; 8:18, 22, 31). Nothing but the blessing of God can explain how an obscure Jewish priest and scholar, born in Babylonian Captivity, could accomplish so much for God and Israel when so much was working against him.

That God's good hand was upon this man doesn't minimize the importance of his personal piety or his great ability as a scholar, nor does it ignore the great help King Artaxerxes gave him.[2] God uses all kinds of people to accomplish His will, but if God's hand isn't at work in us and

35

through us, nothing will be accomplished. It's the principle Jesus taught His disciples, "Without Me you can do nothing" (John 15:5, NKJV). What did God do for the people of Israel during those difficult days after the Babylonian Captivity?

1. He raised up a godly leader (Ezra 7:1-6, 10)

It was the year 458 and Artaxerxes I was King of Persia (465–424). Nearly sixty years had passed since the completion of the temple in Jerusalem, and the Jewish remnant was having a very difficult time. It was then that God raised up Ezra to lead a second group of refugees from Babylon to Judah to bring financial and spiritual support to the work and to help rebuild the city.

Every person is important to God and God's work; but, as Dr. Lee Roberson has often said, "Everything rises and falls with leadership." When God wanted to deliver Israel from Egypt, He raised up Moses and Aaron. When Israel was divided and defeated, He called Samuel to teach the Word and David to serve as king. Richard Nixon was right when he said that leaders are people who "make a difference,"[3] and Ezra was that kind of man.

When God wants to judge a nation, He sends them inferior leaders (Isa. 3:1-8); but when He wants to bless them, He sends them men like Ezra.

His noble ancestry (Ezra 7:1-5). There were some priests in the Jewish remnant who couldn't prove their ancestry (2:61-63), but Ezra wasn't among them. He had the best of credentials and could prove his lineage all the way back to Aaron, the first high priest. Some famous spiritual leaders are named in this genealogy, men like Hilkiah, Zadok, and Phineas.[4] Of course, being blessed with godly ancestors is no guarantee of success for their descendants, but it's a good beginning. God promises to bless the descendants of the godly (Deut. 4:40; Ps. 128). "I don't know who my grandfather was," said Abraham Lincoln; "I am much more concerned what his grandson will be." Ezra knew the names of his ancestors and what these men had done, and he made the most of his heritage. He didn't squander the rich spiritual legacy they had entrusted to him but used it to honor the Lord and serve His people. What a tragedy it is when the descendants of godly families turn away from the Lord and lead lives of disobedience and rebellion (Jud. 2:10-15).

His remarkable audacity (Ezra 7:6). You wouldn't expect a priest and scholar like Ezra to dare to approach a mighty king and ask for permission to take a group of Jewish exiles to Jerusalem. Most scholars are retiring by nature, happy with their books and thoughts, and unwilling to get involved in the everyday affairs of life. The American poet and professor Archibald MacLeish wrote, "The scholar digs his ivory cellar in the ruins of the past and lets the present sicken as it will." But not Ezra!

Ezra's careful study of the Word of God had increased his faith (Rom. 10:17) and helped him understand God's plans for the Jewish remnant, and he wanted to be a part of those plans. Certainly as he studied the Old Testament Scriptures, he prayed for God to help His people; and God answered that prayer by calling him to go to Jerusalem. He gave Ezra the boldness to approach the king and the king a desire to cooperate with Ezra's requests.

When the first group of Jews left for Jerusalem in 537, it was because God moved upon the heart of Cyrus (Ezra 1:1-4); but now it was a lowly priest whom God used to touch the heart of King Artaxerxes.

His exceptional ability (7:10). When you recall that Ezra was born in Babylon, you can better appreciate his achievement as a skilled student of the Jewish Scriptures. Undoubtedly, some of the priests had brought copies of the Old Testament scrolls with them to Babylon, and these became very precious to the exiled spiritual leaders of the nation. There was no Jewish temple in Babylon, so the priests and Levites weren't obligated to minister, but some of them, like Ezra, devoted themselves to the study and teaching of the Word of God. [5]

When it comes to our relationship to the Word of God, Ezra is a good example for us to follow. He was a man with a prepared heart, devoted to the study of the Scriptures. "For Ezra had set his heart to study the law of the Lord" (v. 10, NASB). He would have agreed with the psalmist who wrote, "Oh, how I love Your law! It is my meditation all the day" (Ps. 119:97, NKJV). Even the king recognized and affirmed Ezra's great knowledge of the Scriptures (Ezra 7:11-14).

But Ezra did more than study the Word of God; he also practiced it in his daily life. It's in the obeying of the Word that we experience the blessing, not in the reading or the hearing of it (James 1:22-25). "This one is blessed in *what he does*" (v. 25, NKJV, italics added), not in what he thinks he knows. If our knowledge of the truth doesn't result in obedience, then we end up with a big head instead of a burning heart (1 Cor. 8:1; Luke 24:32); and truth becomes a toy to play with, not a tool to build with. Instead of building our Christian character, we only deceive ourselves and try to deceive others (1 John 1:5-10).

Ezra not only studied and obeyed the Word of God, but he also taught it to others. The priests and Levites were commanded by God to be teachers in Israel (Lev. 10:8-11; Deut. 33:10; Mal. 2:7), because that was the only way the people could learn God's truth. The common people couldn't afford to own scrolls of the Law, so it was up to the priests and Levites to read and explain the Scriptures to the people. "So they read in the book in the law of God distinctly, and gave the sense, and caused them to understand the reading" (Neh. 8:8). What a model for all preachers and teachers of the Bible to follow!

Each generation needs to discover the precious treasure of the Word of God, but that can't happen unless previous generations are faithful to learn the Word, guard it, obey it, and teach it. "And the things you have heard me say in the presence of many witnesses entrust to reliable men who will also be qualified to teach others" (2 Tim. 2:2, NIV).[6]

The three qualities mentioned in Ezra 7:10 are paralleled in our Lord's words in Matthew 13:52—"Therefore every scribe who has become a disciple of the kingdom of heaven is like a head of a household, who brings forth out of his treasure things new and old" (NASB). Ezra was a scribe who studied the Word, a disciple who obeyed and practiced the Word, and a householder who shared the Word with others. He's a good example for us to follow.

[Ezra 7:7-9 gives a summary of the journey to Jerusalem, the details of which we will study later.]

2. He directed a pagan ruler (Ezra 7:11-28)

Just as God had worked in the heart and mind of Cyrus (1:1-4) and Darius (6:1-12), so He moved upon Artaxerxes I to permit Ezra and his people to return to their land. After hearing Ezra's requests, Artaxerxes took several steps to assist the Jews in this important undertaking.

Authorization (7:11-12, 25-26). First, Artaxerxes appointed Ezra as the leader of the group and also as the king's agent in Judah, even to the extent of giving him the right to inflict capital punishment on offenders (v. 26). From the way the king described Ezra in his official letter, it's clear that he was impressed with this Jewish priest-scribe and the Law which was the center of his life and ministry. The references to the law of God being in Ezra's hand (vv. 14, 25) may refer to actual scrolls that Ezra brought with him for his audience with the king, or perhaps it simply means "which you possess" (see v. 25, NIV).

Liberation (vv. 13-14). In his official letter, Artaxerxes gave the Jews the privilege to leave Babylon and go to Jerusalem with Ezra and join the remnant in rebuilding the city walls (4:12). Refer back to Ezra 4:7-23 for the account of the trials the Jews had in spite of the king's encouragement, and keep in mind that it was the rebuilding of the city, not the temple, that was involved, along with the spiritual restoration of the people. (See the suggested outline of the Book of Ezra.)

In 537, the first wave of Jewish refugees, about 50,000 of them, returned to Jerusalem under Zerubbabel's leadership to rebuild the temple. Now, in 458, Ezra was authorized to lead the second group, 1,500 men plus women and children, to help restore the walls and gates and to bring spiritual renewal to the people.

In 444, Nehemiah would arrive and finish the job of building the walls and hanging the gates.

Compensation (7:15-26). The Lord had told the struggling people in Jerusalem, "The silver is Mine, and the gold is Mine" (Hag. 2:8, NKJV), and now He proved it by opening the royal treasury and providing money to buy sacrifices to be offered at the temple in Jerusalem. The king commanded his officers beyond the river to give the Jews money out of the local royal treasury and defined the limits (Ezra 7:22). A hundred talents of silver would be nearly four tons of silver!

Then Artaxerxes gave Ezra the sacred articles from the original temple that hadn't been carried back by Zerubbabel (v. 19). Finally, he allowed Ezra to receive gifts from the Jews who remained in Babylon and from anybody else in the realm who wanted to contribute (see 1:4). Not every Jew wanted to go back, and not all were able; but all could contribute something to the work.

Like Darius before him (6:10), Artaxerxes was anxious that the God of Israel bless him and his sons and give success to his kingdom (7:23); so his generosity had somewhat of a selfish motive behind it. But it's doubtful if any person, king or commoner, ever does anything from an absolutely pure motive. It was remarkable that a pagan ruler would be this generous toward a captive people from whom he could hope to gain nothing. After all, if the God of Israel hadn't been able to protect the Jews from Babylonian Captivity, what could He do to help the Persians?

What Artaxerxes did for the Jews was clearly because of the good hand of God that was at work on behalf of God's chosen people. Finally, Artaxerxes exempted the priests, Levites, and temple servants from paying taxes or being conscripted for special duty to the empire (v. 24). Even if he had selfish motives, Artaxerxes was concerned that the temple ministry be strong and steady. To make certain that everything went smoothly as the Jews rebuilt the city, the king gave Ezra extensive authority to enforce the law (v. 26).

Celebration (vv. 27-28). This is the first occurrence of first-person narrative in the book; it continues through 9:15. He praises the Lord for moving the king to cooperate with his plans, and he sees this event as proof of God's mercy or covenant love. Ezra took no credit for this accomplishment; it was all the result of the "good hand of God" upon him. Without wasting any time, he assembled the chief men of the tribes and gathered the people who felt moved to travel to Jerusalem.

3. He gathered a willing remnant (Ezra 8:1-30)

Many of the Jews were comfortable in Mesopotamia and quite satisfied to live and die there. During the Captivity, they had followed Jeremiah's counsel to be good citizens and settle down to normal lives (Jer. 29:1-7). Over the decades, the old generation had died and a new generation had arisen that had never seen Jerusalem or the temple and probably had little interest in the welfare of their fellow Jews sacrificially laboring there. No doubt some of the Jewish men were in government employ or in business and were unable to relocate without paying a great price. Even our Lord had a problem enlisting disciples who were too settled in their successful lifestyles (Luke 9:57-62), and that explains why there's still a shortage of laborers (10:2).

Recruiting (Ezra 8:1-20). Wisely, Ezra gathered eighteen men who were the heads of Jewish families, knowing that they could influence their relatives, and the result was a total of 1,515 men, plus women and children (v. 21), who agreed to go with Ezra to Jerusalem. It wasn't as large a company as the first contingent that had gone with Zerubbabel and Joshua nearly eighty years before, but that didn't discourage them. If you compare the names in this list with those in Ezra 2:3-15, you'll see that many of Ezra's companions were related to those first settlers. The pioneer spirit seems to run in families.

The group left Babylon on the first day of the fifth month (7:9) and after about a week of travel stopped at the River Ahava (probably a canal) for three days before proceeding (8:15, 31). During that time, Ezra took inventory of the people and discovered that there were no Levites going with them,[7] so he sent a special committee of eleven leading men to recruit some Levites for the journey. The committee returned with only 38 Levites, but 220 temple servants came along with them. It's too bad the numbers weren't reversed; but even then, the laborers were few.

Trusting (vv. 21-23). Ezra's whole approach to this trip was a spiritual one; for if the good hand of God wasn't with them, everything would fail. But to receive the blessing and help of God, they had to humble themselves and seek His face, so Ezra called for three days of fasting and prayer, asking God to protect them on their long journey.

Ezra could have asked for an armed escort, but he felt that a request for protection would dishonor the Lord in the eyes of the pagan king. He had already told Artaxerxes that God's good hand was upon him and the Jews, so how could he then ask for human help? Ezra was relying on God's covenant with Abraham (Gen. 12:1-3), that those who bless the Jews are blessed by God, and there's a fine line between faith and presumption. Fourteen years later, Nehemiah didn't hesitate to request an armed escort from the king (Neh. 2:9); and Paul was glad for the Roman soldiers who protected him during his journey from Jerusalem to Caesarea (Acts 23). Were they less devoted than Ezra? Of course not! Undoubtedly the Lord gave Ezra special faith for this journey because He knew that Ezra's desire was only to glorify God. When you consider the factors involved in this expedition, you can see what great faith Ezra possessed. Here were several thousand Jews, inexperienced in travel and warfare, carrying a fortune in gold and silver, led by a scholar, not a soldier, and planning to travel through dangerous territory that was infested with brigands, and yet their leader didn't want an army to protect them! If anybody deserves the "Great Faith Award," it's Ezra!

Committing (Ezra 8:24-30). To twelve leading priests, Ezra committed the responsibility for the treasure: twenty-five tons of silver, nearly eight tons of silver and gold vessels, plus various other vessels and the offering given by the people. The twelve men represented the twelve tribes of Israel and had an obligation to them, but even more, it was the Lord's treasure and these priests would one day give an accounting to Him.

In one sense, this event is a parable of the Christian life. God's people are on a difficult and dangerous journey to the heavenly Jerusalem (Heb. 12:22), and the Lord has committed certain of His treasures to us. Our task is to protect what

He's given us and be ready to give a good account of our stewardship when we get to the end of the journey. The only difference is that, in our journey, God expects us to invest and increase the treasure and not just guard it. (See Matt. 25:14-30; 1 Tim. 1:11, 18-19; 6:20; 2 Tim. 1:13-14; 2:2.)

4. He gave them a safe journey (Ezra 8:31-36)
As these Jewish èmigrès trudged through the wilderness, I wonder if they sang Psalm 121 to each other?

> I will lift up my eyes to the hills—
> From whence comes my help?
> My help comes from the Lord,
> who made heaven and earth.
> He will not allow your foot to be moved;
> He who keeps you will not slumber.
> Behold, He who keeps Israel
> shall neither slumber nor sleep.
> (Ps. 121:1-4, NKJV)

Arriving (Ezra 8:31). They left Babylon on the first day of the first month (7:9), tarried three days at the Ahava canal (8:15), and then left that encampment on the twelfth day of the first month (8:31), arriving at Jerusalem on the first day of the fifth month (7:9). They covered at least 900 miles in four months' time, and the good hand of God protected them and their possessions all the way.

Our God is the Alpha and the Omega; what He starts, He finishes (Rev. 1:8, 11; 21:6; 22:13; Isa. 41:4; 44:6). If God is at the beginning of the journey and we trust Him, He'll remain with us throughout the journey and take us to our destination. Each step of the way, God will see to it that we fulfill His loving purposes; and He will never forsake us (Isa. 43:1-2; Heb. 13:5-6).

Resting (Ezra 8:32). When my wife and I arrive home

from an extended ministry trip, we find that it takes a couple of days to get rested and ready for the next assignment. Perhaps Ezra and his company arrived just before the Sabbath and wisely decided to prolong their rest. Sometimes the most spiritual thing we can do is to do nothing. Jesus told His busy disciples, "Come aside by yourselves to a deserted place and rest a while" (Mark 6:31, NKJV). As Vance Havner used to say, "If you don't come apart, you will come apart—you'll go to pieces."

Reckoning (Ezra 8:33-34). The priests took the treasure to the temple where it was weighed and inventoried, and all the facts were written down so an official report could be sent to the king. "Let all things be done decently and in order" (1 Cor. 14:40). God's servants must be faithful in every area of ministry, but especially in the matter of money. When you read 2 Corinthians 8–9, you see how scrupulous Paul and his associates were in handling the "relief offering" that the Gentile churches were sending to Jerusalem. "For we are taking pains to do what is right, not only in the eyes of the Lord but also in the eyes of men" (2 Cor. 8:21).

Worshiping (Ezra 8:35). The Jewish residents and the new arrivals gathered at the altar to worship God and declare their unity as His people. The twelve burnt offerings and twelve sin offerings were for the twelve tribes of Israel represented by the Jewish remnant in Jerusalem. Unlike the initial worship over seventy-five years before, when the altar was first set up, there's no record of anybody lamenting for "the good old days" (3:11-13).

The new arrivals were worshiping in their land, at their temple altar, for the first time in their lives! How Ezra's heart must have been stirred as he stood at the altar and participated in the worship service! "I was glad when they said to me, 'Let us go into the house of the Lord.' Our feet have been standing within your gates, O Jerusalem!" (Ps. 122:1-2, NKJV)

Clearance (Ezra 8:36). Having taken care of the spiritual matters that related to the nation and the temple, Ezra then presented himself and his credentials to the local Persian officials. "Render therefore to Caesar the things that are Caesar's, and to God the things that are God's" (Luke 20:25). He gave them the king's letter, and the officers were quick to obey the king's orders and assist the Jews in their projects. Ezra left Babylon with God's law in his heart and the king's letter in his hand and the good hand of God upon him. No wonder his mission was a success.

F O U R

The Grace of God

Ezra must have experienced great joy and satisfaction when he found himself in the Holy City, worshiping at the restored temple and ministering to the spiritual needs of the people. He certainly would have had an easier life had he remained "Scholar in Residence" for the exiles in Babylon, but "an easier life" wasn't on Ezra's agenda. God had called him to serve the Jewish remnant and teach them the Law of God, and he was obedient to God's call.

But four months after his arrival (7:9; 10:9), he learned that all wasn't well in Jerusalem because over 100 civil and religious leaders of the nation were guilty of deliberately disobeying the Law that Ezra had come to teach. How Ezra faced this difficult problem and solved it is an example for any Christian today who takes seriously God's repeated command, "You shall be holy; for I am holy" (Lev. 11:44, NKJV).[1]

1. Contamination: A sinful people (Ezra 9:1-2)

A group of laypeople informed Ezra that some of the leaders of the tribes, as well as some priests and Levites, had taken foreign wives for themselves and for their sons, and some of

47

these men had even divorced their Jewish wives in order to marry heathen women (Mal. 2:10-16).

It was perfectly in order for these concerned Jews to report to Ezra what was going on, for he was one of their key spiritual leaders and carried great authority from the king (Ezra 7:25-26). It's likely that these concerned citizens had opposed the mixed marriages but were ignored, so they appealed to their leading priest and scribe for his help. The household of Chloe had informed Paul about some of the flagrant sins in the church at Corinth (1 Cor. 1:11), and he didn't rebuke them for it because there's a difference between "religious gossip" and honest concern. Covering sin never brings blessing to a nation or an individual (Prov. 28:13; see Deut. 17:1-7).

Disobedience (Ezra 9:1). The actions of these Jewish men were in violation of the Law of God (Ex. 34:15-16; Deut. 7:1-6). As the Book of Ruth testifies, it was legal for a Jewish man to marry a foreign woman if she fully renounced her old life and accepted her husband's faith; but this law didn't apply to the women native to the land of Canaan. According to Deuteronomy 20:1-15 and 21:10-14, a Jewish soldier could marry a female prisoner of war from a distant city, but he was forbidden to marry a Canaanite woman. But, when people decide to deliberately disobey the Word of God, they can usually find excuses to defend their actions. "There's a shortage of unmarried Jewish women," they might argue, "and we need to keep our families' names alive and help to increase the population." In other words, the end justifies the means. Blame the single Jewish women who wouldn't leave Babylon!

Did anyone offer to return to Babylon to find eligible wives for these single men?

Defilement (Ezra 9:2). God gave that marriage law to Israel in order to protect the nation from defilement.

Because of these mixed marriages, the "holy seed" ("race," NIV) was being defiled by foreign women from the very nations God had commanded Israel to destroy (Deut. 7:1-6). The Jews weren't called a "holy nation" (Ex. 19:5-6) because they were better than anybody else, but because God had chosen them in His love and set them apart to do His will (Deut. 7:7-11). It's through Israel that "all families of the earth [shall be] blessed" (Gen. 12:3; 28:14), for the Jews gave the world three wonderful gifts: the knowledge of the true and living God, the written Word of God, and the Savior, Jesus Christ.

If it was wicked for single Jewish men to marry foreign women, how much greater was the guilt of married men who divorced their Jewish wives in order to marry pagan women! The Prophet Malachi denounced the Jewish men who did this (Mal. 2:13-16) and reminded them that Jehovah was seeking "a godly seed" (Ezra 9:15, KJV; "offspring," NIV, NKJV). This could refer to the promised Messiah as well as the future generations of Jews (Isa. 6:12-13). How could the Jews keep their nation "holy" if the men married out of the will of God? If the leaders of Israel continued to set such a bad example in defiling themselves, they would also defile the nation; and it wouldn't take long for Israel to lose their separated position in the world. Like Solomon (1 Kings 11), the men would start adopting the false gods and evil practices of their heathen wives; and before long, the true faith would be destroyed (Ex. 34:10-16). How then could God bring the Savior into the world? [2]

2. Concern: a privileged people (Ezra 9:3-15) [3]
How privileged the remnant was to have a spiritual leader like Ezra! He had been given special authority by the king (7:25-26), so you can see how serious it was for him to know what these men had done. Depending on the offense, Ezra

could banish people from the community, confiscate their wealth, or even order their execution! But Ezra was first of all a man of God who sought God's best for his people, and he identified with them and made their burdens his burdens. He was supremely a man of prayer.

He didn't preach a sermon, although they needed to be reminded of what the Law said, nor did he immediately seek out the sinners and call them to confession and repentance, as important as that was. The first thing he did was to go to the temple, sit on the ground and express his grief before the people and before the Lord. As though he were mourning the dead, he tore his tunic and his cloak (9:5; see Gen. 37:29, 34; Josh. 7:6), and in further expression of sorrow, he plucked out hair from his head and his beard.[4] The people saw this and it reached their hearts.

Ezra was "appalled" (Ezra 9:3, NIV). The Hebrew word means "to be shocked, horrified, astonished, desolate." How could these men who were sons of the covenant commit such heinous sins? They had been so wonderfully helped by God in being freed from bondage and allowed to return to their land, and now they had rebelled against the Lord who had blessed them so much! And some of the offenders were priests and Levites who certainly knew the Law!

One of the maladies of society today is that people are no longer shocked by sin and willing to do something about it. Political leaders can flagrantly break the law and not only get away with it but be admired by the public and be elected to office again. Polls indicate that many Americans don't consider "character" to be an important factor when it comes to choosing leaders. In spite of all the noise about "religious revival" and "megachurches," God's people don't seem to be functioning well as salt and light in society. The salt has lost its flavor and no longer stings and prevents corruption, and the light is hidden under a bushel (Matt. 5:13-16).

During the time that Ezra sat fasting[5] and mourning, a crowd gathered around him made up of people who "trembled at the words of the God of Israel" (Ezra 9:4; see 10:9). The Jews had trembled greatly at Sinai when God spoke the Word (Ex. 19:16; Heb. 12:21), but later generations simply took God's Word for granted and didn't worry if they disregarded it. Too many Christians today are willing to read the Bible, study it, outline it, and even defend it; but they don't fear God and seek to obey what the Bible says. "But on this one will I look: on him who is poor and of a contrite spirit, and who trembles at My word" (Isa. 66:2, NKJV). Until God's people show respect for God and His Word, the Spirit of God can't work in mighty power as He longs to do.

At three o'clock in the afternoon, when the priests offered the daily evening sacrifice (Num. 28:1-4) and the people were assembling for prayer (Acts 3:1; Ps. 55:17; Dan. 6:10), Ezra began to call out to God and intercede for his people. As he wept (Ezra 10:1) and prayed, perhaps he was thinking of God's promise in 2 Chronicles 7:14, "If My people who are called by My name will humble themselves, and pray and seek My face, and turn from their wicked ways, then I will hear from heaven, and will forgive their sin and heal their land" (NKJV).

"We have sinned" (Ezra 9:5-7). Like both Nehemiah (Neh. 1:4-10) and Daniel (Dan. 9), Ezra identified himself with the people and their sins and spoke to God about "our iniquities" and not "their iniquities." Israel was one covenant nation before God, and the sins of one person affected all the people. For example, when Achan disobeyed God at Jericho, God said to Joshua, "*Israel* has sinned" (Josh. 7:11, NKJV, italics mine). The same principle applies to the local church (1 Cor. 5:6-8). Unless sin is dealt with, the whole assembly becomes defiled.

Like the publican in our Lord's parable (Luke 18:9-14),

Ezra was too ashamed to look up to heaven as he prayed. The inability to blush because of sin is a mark of hypocrisy and superficial spiritual experience (Jer. 6:13-15). "Are they ashamed of their loathsome conduct? No, they have no shame at all; they do not even know how to blush" (Jer. 8:12, NIV). Words and actions that would have made earlier generations blush in shame are today part of the normal "entertainment" diet of the average TV viewer. When a nation turns sin into entertainment and laughs at what ought to make us weep, we are in desperate need of revival.

Why was Ezra so ashamed? *Because his people hadn't learned their lesson from all the trials that the nation had experienced (Ezra 9:7).* The new generation had grown up in Babylon and become so accustomed to the evil around them that they had no true fear of God. They should have been like Paul in Athens, who grieved over the wickedness that he saw (Acts 17:16), but instead, they first accepted Babylon's sinful way of life, then approved of it, and then enjoyed it. This compromising attitude went with them to Jerusalem and eventually revealed itself in their disobedience.

When you read the messages of the Prophet Malachi, you see how backslidden the priests were as they "served God" in the restored temple, and worldly spiritual leaders will produce worldly worshipers. While the older generation of Jews may have learned obedience through the chastening God sent them, the younger generation didn't learn the lessons their elders tried to teach them. The spiritual history of Israel, summarized in Ezra 9:7, is living proof that privileges bring responsibilities, and that much is required from those to whom much is given (Luke 12:48).

"We are unworthy of Your blessings" (Ezra 9:8-9). Ezra used five different images to picture what God's grace had done for the people who had returned to the land. In His

grace, God had preserved a *remnant,* like a piece of cloth torn from a robe and kept safe (see 1 Kings 11:26-40). Throughout Jewish history, even when the nation turned from God, He always preserved a remnant that remained faithful to Him (1 Kings 19:18; Isa. 1:9; Mal. 3:16-17; Luke 2:38); and from that remnant, He made a new beginning.

Ezra then spoke about the *"nail in his holy place."* The image here is that of a nail pounded into the sanctuary wall or a tent peg driven into the ground, and it depicts security and stability, the foothold the Jews now had in their land. God had brought the remnant back to their land and given them favor with the king and the local officials, and had they trusted Him and obeyed His Word, He would have blessed them abundantly. But they chose to go their own way; so He had to chasten them with poor crops, bad weather, and serious economic problems (Hag. 1).

Third, God gave *light to their eyes,* by taking them out of Babylonian Captivity and returning them to their own land. To have your "eyes lightened" speaks of new life, new joy, and the dawning of a new day (Pss. 13:3; 34:5). It's similar to the next image, "to give us a little reviving in our bondage." The presence of the remnant in the land was like a resurrection from the dead! Their departure from Babylon was like the resurrection of a corpse from the grave.

Ezra's final image is that of *"a wall in Judah and in Jerusalem"* (Ezra 9:10), and it speaks of the protection God had given His people. He had worked in the hearts of kings— Cyrus, Darius, Xerxes, and Artaxerxes I—to gain them release from bondage and security in their own land. These were proud powerful rulers, but the Lord in His sovereignty used them to fulfill His purposes.

No wonder Ezra was ashamed. After all God had done for His people, they responded by disobeying His Word. *"We are speechless"* (Ezra 9:10-12). A knowledge of God's Word is indispensable for effective praying (John 15:7), and Ezra knew the Old Testament Scriptures thoroughly. In these verses, he refers to a number of passages from Moses and the prophets, including Leviticus 18:24-26; Deuteronomy 7:1-6 and 11:8-9; Isaiah 1:19; 2 Kings 23:8-16; Ezekiel 5:11 and 37:25. It's obvious that these Jewish men were sinning against a flood of light.

The religious practices of the Canaanites were unspeakably vile and the stench reached to heaven. God had patiently held back His wrath, but the time of their judgment came when Israel invaded the land (Gen. 15:16). Wiping out the Canaanite civilization was like a surgeon removing a cancerous tumor or an engineer stopping a flood of poisonous sewage. Note the words that Ezra used in his prayer: unclean, filthiness, uncleanness, abominations.

God's law made it clear that Israel was to have no association with these nations, and now over 100 Jewish men had taken the first step by marrying into their families (Ezra 9:12). This could, of course, lead to peaceful relations and perhaps even wealth, but what about the future? What would happen to the children of these mixed marriages when it came time to obey God and become a part of the covenant? These men were sacrificing the future and paying a great price to do it. It wasn't worth it. No wonder Ezra was speechless and asked, "What shall we say after this?"

"We are guilty" (vv. 13-15). Guilt always shuts a person's mouth before God (Rom. 3:19). Sinners can give Him no logical reason for their sins and no acceptable excuses. Ezra not only confessed their sins but admitted that God had treated them far better than they deserved. He knew that God could easily destroy the remnant and start again with another people (Ex. 32:10; Num. 14:11-12), but, like Moses, he asked God to be gracious and forgiving.

Nobody could stand in His presence; nobody could speak

in His presence. They were a guilty people, some of them because they deliberately broke God's law, and others because they allowed the offenders to get away with their sins. But God is righteous, and a righteous God must punish sin.

Before we try to untangle the problems of life, we must take time to seek God's face in prayer. This is not a long prayer. It can be read aloud very deliberately in only a few minutes, but it has tremendous depth. Charles Spurgeon used to say that it was the strength of our prayers, not the length of our prayers, that was important; and he was right. When you pray from a burdened heart, with a mind that's saturated with God's Word, then God will hear and answer.

3. Cooperation: a willing people (Ezra 10:1-8)

Never underestimate the power of the prayers of one dedicated believer (James 5:16-18), for the intercession of only one concerned person can make a difference in what God will do to and for His people. As Ezra prayed and wept at the altar before the house of God, "a very great congregation of men and women and children" came together, and they fell under conviction of sin.

"They too wept bitterly" (Ezra 10:1, NIV). This response wasn't something that Ezra worked up; it was something that he prayed down. The priests had offered a lamb on the altar, but Ezra gave the Lord an even greater sacrifice. "The sacrifices of God are a broken spirit, a broken and a contrite heart—these, O God, You will not despise" (Ps. 51:17, NKJV).

As I watch the contemporary religious scene, I note that churches occasionally feature "Christian comedians" and "Christian clowns," but not much is said about people who know how to weep and pray. As much as anyone else, I appreciate a sense of humor and a good laugh, but there comes a time when God's people need to stop laughing and start weeping and confessing. "Lament and mourn and weep! Let your laughter be turned to mourning and your joy to gloom. Humble yourselves in the sight of the Lord, and He will lift you up" (James 4:9-10, NKJV). That's God's formula for revival.

Shecaniah was the spokesman for the people, a man whose own relatives had sinned by marrying foreign women (Ezra 10:26). In my pastoral ministry, I've seen churches split and their witness almost destroyed because people have sided with their disobedient relatives in matters of discipline instead of with the Lord and His Word. Perhaps Shecaniah remembered what Moses wrote about the evils of being partial in judgment (Deut. 13:6-11; 17:1-13). Paul taught this same principle for the local church (1 Tim. 5:21).

To most of the people gathered around Ezra, the situation probably appeared hopeless; but not to Shecaniah, who said, "Yet now there is hope in Israel concerning this thing" (Ezra 10:2). He confessed that he and the rest of the nation were guilty, and then suggested a plan of action.

The plan was simple but demanding. First, the nation would unitedly covenant to obey God's law. Then, Ezra and a group of men who "trembled at the Word" would decide how the matter would be settled; and the people promised to obey whatever was decreed. But everything had to be done according to the Law of Moses.

Ezra accepted the plan. He immediately swore in the leading priests and Levites as the committee to investigate the matter and see to it that the law was obeyed. But instead of participating immediately in the investigation, he withdrew into one of the rooms of the temple to fast and pray for God's guidance. He left it to the special committee to make the decisions and tell the people what to do. Wise is the leader who involves other people in the process, especially when the issue is so sensitive.

The committee issued a proclamation to the people of Jerusalem and of the outlying villages to appear in Jerusalem within three days or be in danger of expulsion from the community. At that time, each marriage would be investigated and the committee would discover who had violated the Mosaic Law.

A humble praying leader, a willing people, and a faithful and courageous committee worked together to accomplish a difficult task. What an example for the church to follow today!

4. Cleansing: an obedient people (Ezra 10:9-44)

On December 19, 458, the men of the two main tribes, Judah and Benjamin, plus exiles from the other tribes, gathered in the street before the temple to start the solemn investigation. (This meeting may have been convened at the Water Gate where Ezra later expounded the Law to the people, Neh. 8:1ff.)

It was December, the middle of the rainy season (October to mid-April), and the crowd trembled, not only because of the weather, but also because they were sure the heavy rain was a prelude to the judgment of God. Ezra made it clear that the mixed marriages would have to be dissolved, and he called upon the faithful Jews to separate themselves from those who had disobeyed God's law.

Once again, Ezra was given counsel by others, and he accepted it. (Blessed is the leader who has open ears to the ideas of others!) It was suggested that Ezra empower the committee of priests and Levites to work with the leaders of the tribes, as well as the elders and judges of the towns (who knew their people), and let them determine who was guilty. It was impractical to try to interrogate so many people in one place, especially when the weather was so inclement; and the work couldn't be done in a day. Except for four men who dissented (Ezra 10:15), the crowd agreed with this idea and promised to obey.

Ten days later (v. 16), on December 29, Ezra and the leaders sat down together and began to investigate the matter; three months later, on March 27, 457, their work was finished. It must have been a difficult job to do, but they persisted with the help of the Lord. They discovered over 100 offenders,[6] including 27 priests, Levites, temple singers, and gatekeepers, people you would have expected to be models of obedience.

When spiritual leaders begin to sin, it doesn't take long for other people to follow. While we don't want to minimize the enormity of the sin, it should be noted that the number of offenders was very low when compared to the size of the population. Eighty years before, nearly 50,000 Jews had returned with Zerubbabel and Joshua, and during the ensuing years, the people surely multiplied. The total number of offenders was probably less than 1 percent of the residents. However, it's better to deal with these matters when the numbers are low, because the longer you wait, the more the sin will spread. Even one offender is one too many (Ecc. 9:18).

The guilty priests promised to put away their heathen wives, and they offered sacrifices to seek God's forgiveness (Ezra 10:18-19). We assume that the other offenders listed followed their example. God in His grace accepted their repentance and confession and granted them forgiveness.

The Book of Ezra opens in chapter 2 with a list of the names of the Jewish heroes who willingly returned to the land to serve the Lord. The book ends with a list of the sinners who disobeyed God but publicly made it right with the Lord and the people. But "making it right" didn't automatically heal every wound or remove every pain, because the women involved had to leave the community and go back to the heathen homes from which they had come, taking with them whatever children had been born to the union. It's easy to pull the nails out of the board, but it's impossible to pull out the holes that they leave behind.

Over thirteen years later, the problem of mixed marriages appeared again while Nehemiah was governor of Jerusalem (Neh. 13:23-31). It's possible for leaders to enforce the law and reform a nation's conduct, but only God can change the human heart and produce the kind of character that wants to do what's right. That's the difference between "reformation" and "revival."

Now we turn to the Prophet Haggai whose ministry helped to make the rebuilding of the temple possible.

Haggai in His Time

While their names aren't in the official lists, the Prophets Haggai and Zechariah were probably among the nearly 50,000 Jewish exiles who left Babylon for Judah in 537, encouraged by the edict of King Cyrus (Ezra 1:1-4; 5:1-2; 6:14). Haggai 2:3 suggests that Haggai had seen Solomon's temple before it was destroyed and therefore was an old man, while Zechariah is called a young man (Zech. 2:4). These two prophets belonged to different generations, but this didn't hinder them from working together to get the temple rebuilt.

We know nothing about Haggai's family background, call, or personal life. When the work on the temple had been stopped for sixteen years (536–520), Haggai and Zechariah suddenly began to preach and to encourage the people to put God first and get back to work (Hag. 1:1; Zech. 1:1).

Haggai's book is the second shortest in the Old Testament (Obad. is first) and consists of four messages he gave over a period of five months in the year 520 (Hag. 1:1; 2:1, 10, 20). He called the people to "consider" (1:5, 7; 2:15, 18, NIV, "give careful thought") and realize what it was costing them to neglect God's house. Certainly he was reminding them of God's covenant promises recorded in Deuteronomy 28. But he also encouraged them by assuring them that God was with them in their work (Hag. 1:13; 2:4).

The temple was completed in 515, so Haggai and Zechariah didn't minister in vain.

A Suggested Outline of the Book of Haggai

Key Theme: Complete the work you have begun
Key verse: Haggai 1:8

I. First message: conviction —1:1-15
    1. Stop making excuses—1-4
    2. Start considering your ways—5-11
    3. Begin to serve the Lord—12-15

II. Second message: comparison —2:1-9
    1. Discouragement—1-3
    2. Encouragement—4-9
        (1) Be strong—4
        (2) Fear not—5
        (3) Glory will come—6-7
        (4) God will provide—8-9

III. Third message: contamination—2:10-19
    1. The question of defilement—10-13
    2. The assurance of blessing—14-19

IV. Fourth message: coronation—2:20-23
    1. The coming judgment—20-22
    2. The promised Messiah—23

Stirring Up God's People

When the foundations of the temple were laid in Jerusalem in the year 536, the younger men shouted for joy while the older men wept (Ezra 3:8-13). Although Haggai probably had seen Solomon's temple in its glory (Hag. 2:3), he was undoubtedly among those who expressed joy, for the Lord was at work among His people.

But it doesn't take long for zeal to cool and God's people to grow apathetic, especially when opposition began an ominous growl that soon became a roar. The shout awakened the enemies of the Jews, aroused official opposition, and caused the work to stop (Ezra 4:1-6, 24); and the temple lay unfinished from 536 to 520, when Haggai and Zechariah brought God's message to Zerubbabel and Joshua.

In this first message, the prophet gave four admonitions to the leaders and to the people to encourage them to get back to work and finish rebuilding the temple.

1. "Put God first in your lives" (Hag. 1:1-4)
The first statement in the divine message went right to the heart of the problem and exposed the hypocrisy and unbelief of the people.

Excuses. "It isn't time to rebuild the house of the Lord" was their defense of their inactivity. Billy Sunday called an excuse "the skin of a reason stuffed with a lie," and Benjamin Franklin wrote, "I never knew a man who was good at making excuses who was good at anything else."

The first congregation I pastored met in a corrugated metal tabernacle that should have been replaced years before, but whenever somebody would suggest a building program, some of the fearful people would resurrect their excuses for maintaining the status quo. "The economy isn't good and there might be another strike," was the major excuse we heard, but in that part of the country, there were always strikes! And who can predict or control the economy? "Our pastors don't stay long," one member told me, "and it would be a tragedy to be in a building program without a leader." But the Lord led us to build a lovely sanctuary and He saw us through!

Evidence. What more evidence did the Jewish people need that God's time had come? How could they doubt that it was God's will for them to rebuild the temple and restore true worship in Jerusalem? Hadn't God moved King Cyrus to free the exiles and commission them to return to Jerusalem for that very purpose? (See 2 Chron. 36:22-23; Ezra 1:1-4.) Didn't the king generously give them the money and materials they needed, and didn't the Lord graciously protect the exiles carrying the temple treasures as they traveled from Babylon to Judah?

The Jews certainly knew the words that the Prophet Isaiah had recorded about Cyrus: "He is My shepherd, and he shall perform all My pleasure, even saying to Jerusalem, 'You shall be rebuilt,' and the temple, 'Your foundation shall be laid' "(Isa. 44:28, NKJV). Isaiah had also written, "I have raised him [Cyrus] up in righteousness, and I will direct all his ways; he shall build My city and let My exiles go free"

(Isa. 45:13). By stopping their work, the Jews were admitting that they had no faith in God's Word or in God's power to perform it.

In the light of these facts, on what basis were the people refusing to obey God and build His house? For one thing, both Isaiah and Jeremiah had predicted a national restoration that would amaze the Gentile nations and bring glory to Israel, but that wonderful event had not yet occurred. (See Isa. 2:1-5; 11; 35; 60:1-5; Jer. 30–31.) The people failed to understand that some of these promises would be fulfilled in the end times ("the last days"); and when the situation in Judah became worse, the people questioned the dependability of the Word of God.

Perhaps some of the scribes studied Jeremiah's promise about the seventy years of captivity (25:1-14) and decided that the allotted time hadn't yet ended. Only fifty years had transpired since the temple had been destroyed in 586, said the experts, so the Jews would have to wait another twenty years for the prophecy to be fulfilled. God took them at their word, and the work stopped for sixteen years. The temple was completed in 515, so the scholars got their seventy years accounted for!

Evasion. The people were terribly inconsistent: it wasn't time to build the house of God, *but it was time to build their own houses!* And some of the people had built, not just ordinary dwellings, but "paneled houses," the kind that kings built for themselves (1 Kings 7:3, 7; Jer. 22:14).

"But seek first the kingdom of God and His righteousness, and all these things [food, clothing, shelter] shall be added to you" (Matt. 6:33, NKJV). Haggai's congregation had never heard that great promise, but the principle behind Christ's words was written into their Law. "Honor the Lord with your possessions, and with the firstfruits of all your increase; so your barns will be filled with plenty, and your vats will overflow with new wine" (Prov. 3:9-10, NKJV; and see Lev. 26:3-13; Deut. 16:17; 28:1-14; 30:3-9).

It's obvious that the nation had its priorities confused, but are God's people today any different from those ancient Jews?

Local churches can't expand their budgets for world evangelism because the money isn't there, and yet many church members don't believe Matthew 6:33 and put God first in their giving. Measured by Third World standards, Christians in the Western world are living in luxury, yet their giving is low and their debts are high because their wealth is being used for things that really don't matter.

When we put God first and give Him what's rightfully His, we open the door to spiritual enrichment and the kind of stewardship that honors the Lord. A century after Haggai ministered, the Prophet Malachi accused the people of robbing God of tithes and offerings and thereby robbing themselves of blessing (Mal. 3:7-12); and his words need to be heeded today.

2. "Believe God's promises" (Hag. 1:5-6, 9-11)

Haggai's second admonition invited the people to examine their lifestyle and actions in the light of the covenant God made with them before the nation entered the land of Canaan (Lev. 26; Deut. 27–28). The word translated "consider" in the KJV is translated "give careful thought to" in the NIV (Hag. 1:5). It was time for the people to do some serious self-examination before the Lord.

God's covenant stated clearly that He would bless them if they obeyed His Law and discipline them if they disobeyed. "If you do not obey Me, then I will punish you seven times more for your sins. I will break the pride of your power; I will make your heavens like iron and your earth like bronze. And your strength shall be spent in vain; for your land shall not yield its produce, nor shall the trees of the land yield their fruit" (Lev. 26:18-20; see Deut. 28:38-40).

Indeed, their strength was spent in vain! They sowed abundantly but reaped a meager harvest. When they ate and drank, they weren't filled or satisfied. Their clothing didn't keep them warm and their income didn't cover their expenses. As supplies became scarcer, prices got higher, and a shopper might as well have carried his wealth in a wallet filled with holes!

While I don't believe that the Old Testament tithe is demanded of the New Testament believer (Acts 5:1-4), I think that tithing is a good place to start when it comes to systematic stewardship. After all, if an Old Covenant Jew under Law could gladly give tithes to the Lord, should a New Covenant believer under grace do less? But the tithe is only a start! The principles laid down in 2 Corinthians 8–9 encourage us to give offerings to the Lord and trust Him for all that we need (see 2 Cor. 8:9).

Because the Jews returned to the land in obedience to the Lord, they thought He would give them special blessings because of their sacrifices, but they were disappointed (Hag. 1:9). Instead, the Lord called for a drought and withheld both the dew and the rain. He took His blessing away from the men who labored in the fields, vineyards, and orchards. In verse 11, Haggai named the basic products that the people needed to survive: water, grain, wine, and oil (Deut. 7:13; 11:14).

Once more, the prophet revealed the source of their trouble: the people were busy building their own houses and had no time for the house of the Lord (Hag. 1:9). It's Matthew 6:33 all over again! Had the nation believed what God promised in His covenants, they would have obeyed Him and enjoyed His blessing.

However, we must be careful not to turn giving into a

"business arrangement," for our obedience should be the evidence of our love and faith. Christian industrialist R.G. LeTourneau used to say, "If you give because it pays, it won't pay!" He was right.

The Lord never made a "prosperity covenant" with the church as He did with Israel. In fact, our Lord's first statement in the Sermon on the Mount is, "Blessed are the poor in spirit, for theirs is the kingdom of heaven" (Matt. 5:3). "Blessed are you poor, for yours is the kingdom of God" (Luke 6:20). God has seen fit to bless some Christians with wealth, but it isn't a guarantee for every believer, in spite of what the contemporary "prosperity preachers" claim. If we help to meet the needs of others, God does promise to meet our needs (Phil. 4:10-20; 2 Cor. 9:6-1), but this isn't a pledge of material prosperity. No matter how much God gives us materially, we all must say with Paul, "as poor, yet making many rich" (2 Cor. 6:10).

3. "Honor God's name" (Hag. 1:7-8)

When the Babylonian army set fire to the temple, this destroyed the great timbers that helped to hold the massive stonework together. The stones were still usable, but the interior woodwork had been demolished and burned and had to be replaced.

According to Ezra 3:7, the Jews purchased wood from Tyre and Sidon, just as Solomon had done when he built the original temple (1 Kings 5:6-12). Now Haggai commanded the men to go into the forests on the mountains and cut down timber to be used for repairing and rebuilding the temple. What happened to that original supply of wood? Did the people use it for themselves? Did some clever entrepreneur profit by selling wood that had been bought with the king's grant? We don't know, but we wonder where the people got the wood for their paneled houses when no wood was available for God's house.

During nearly fifty years of ministry, I've noted that some professed Christians buy the best for themselves and give to the Lord whatever is left over. Worn-out furniture is given to the church and worn-out clothing is sent to the missionaries. Like the priests in Malachi's day, we bring to the Lord gifts we'd be embarrassed to give to our family and friends (Mal. 1:6-8). But when we do this, we commit two sins: (1) we displease the Lord, and (2) we disgrace His name. The Lord told the people through Haggai, "Build the house, so that I may take pleasure in it and be honored" (Hag. 1:7). God delights in the obedient service of His people, and His name is glorified when we sacrifice for Him and serve Him.[2]

"Hallowed be Thy name" is the first petition in the Lord's Prayer (Matt. 6:9), but it's often the last thing we think about as we seek to serve God. Jesus said, "I do always those things that please Him [the Father]" (John 8:29), and that's a good example for us to follow. "Let your light so shine before men, that they may see your good works, and glorify your Father, who is in heaven" (Matt. 5:16).

It certainly didn't please God or honor His name when the people neglected God's house and built elaborate houses for themselves. We know that God doesn't live in temples made by hands (Acts 7:48-50), and that our church buildings are not His holy habitation, but the way we care for these buildings reflects our spiritual priorities and our love for Him. Dr. G. Campbell Morgan said it best in a sermon he preached on Haggai 1:4 many years ago:

Whereas the house of God today is no longer material but spiritual, the material is still a very real symbol of the spiritual. When the Church of God in any place in any locality is careless about the material place of assembly, the place of its worship and its work, it is a sign and evidence that its life is at a low ebb.[3]

4. "Obey His command" (Hag. 1:12-15)

When God speaks to us by His Word, there's only one acceptable response, and that's obedience. We don't weigh the options, we don't examine the alternatives, and we don't negotiate the terms. We simply do what God tells us to do and leave the rest with Him. "Faith is not believing in spite of evidence," said the British preacher Geoffrey Studdert-Kennedy; "it's obeying in spite of consequence."

The leaders and all the people united in obeying God's instructions, and they were motivated by a reverent fear of the Lord (v. 12). After all, He is the "Lord of hosts," a title used ten times in this little book (vv. 2, 9, 14; 2:4, 7, 8, 9, 23). It means "the Lord of the armies," the God who is in supreme command of the armies of heaven (stars and angels) and of earth.[4] Obedience always brings further truth (John 7:17), and the prophet assured them that God was with them in their endeavors (Hag. 1:13; see 2:4). "The Lord of hosts is with us; the God of Jacob is our refuge" (Ps. 46:7, 11). The obedience of the leaders and people was the result of God working in their hearts, just as He had worked in the heart of King Cyrus and in the hearts of the exiles who had returned to Jerusalem with Zerubbabel (Ezra 1:5). "For it is God who works in you both to will and to do for His good pleasure" (Phil. 2:13, NKJV).

Haggai delivered this first message on August 29, 520, but it wasn't until September 21 that the people resumed their work on the temple. Why the three-week delay? For one thing, it was the month when figs and grapes were harvested, and the people didn't want to lose their crop. Also, before they could build, the Jews had to remove the debris from the temple site, take inventory of their supplies, and organize their work crews. It would have been foolish to rush ahead totally unprepared. It's also possible that they took time to confess their sins and purify themselves so that their work would be pleasing to the Lord (Ps. 51:16-19).

The church today can learn a lesson from the Jewish remnant of Haggai's day. Too often we make excuses when we ought to be making confessions and obeying the Lord. We say, "It's not time for an evangelistic crusade," "It's not time for the Spirit to bring revival," "It's not time to expand the ministry." We act as though we fully understand "the times and the seasons" that God has ordained for His people, but we don't understand them (Acts 1:6-7).

Any interpretation of the Bible that limits God and encourages His people to be lazy instead of busy in ministry is a false interpretation and must be abandoned. If the Lord is to be pleased with us and glorified before an unbelieving world, we must hear His Word, believe it, and act upon it, no matter what the circumstances may be. After all, God is with us, and "If God be for us, who can be against us?" (Rom. 8:31)

S I X

Keeping the Work Alive

It's one thing to get God's people back to work and quite another thing to keep them on the job. Dr. Bob Jones, Sr. often said that the greatest ability a person can possess is dependability but too often potential workers excuse themselves and say, "Here am I, Lord; send somebody else." God's pattern for His workers is stated in 1 Corinthians 15:52. "To work is to pray," said St. Augustine, and God's people can do any legitimate task to the glory of God (1 Cor. 10:31).

The rebuilding of the temple was a very special task, for it meant the restoring of true worship in Jerusalem; and completing the project would please the Lord and be a great testimony to the unbelieving nations who were watching the remnant in Jerusalem. Haggai delivered three more brief messages to encourage the laborers to complete their assignments. In each message, he asked them to look in a specific direction to learn what God wanted them to learn.

1. "Look up: God is with us" (Hag. 2:1-9)
When the foundation of the temple had been laid sixteen years before, some of the older men had looked back in sorrow as they remembered the glory and beauty of

71

Solomon's temple (Ezra 3:8-13). It's likely that Haggai was a member of the older generation and had seen the temple before it was destroyed, but he certainly didn't weep with the rest of his peers. He rejoiced that the work had begun, and he wanted to see it completed.

Discouragement (Hag. 2:1-3). Rather than ignore the problem of discouragement that was sure to come when the people contrasted the two temples, the prophet faced the problem head-on. He picked an important day on which to deliver his message: October 17, the last day of the Feast of Tabernacles. This feast was devoted to praising God for the harvest and for remembering Israel's pilgrim days in the wilderness (Lev. 23:34-43).

But the important thing about the date was this: it was during the Feast of Tabernacles that King Solomon had dedicated the original temple (1 Kings 8:2), and Haggai wanted the people to think about that. The restored building had nothing of the splendor of Solomon's temple, but it was still God's house, built according to His plan and for His glory. The same ministry would be performed at its altars and the same worship presented to the Lord. Times change, but ministry goes on.

Encouragement: God's presence (Hag. 2:4-9). Haggai didn't deny that the new temple was "as nothing" in comparison to what Solomon had built, but that wasn't important. The important thing was that this was God's work and they could depend on Him to help them finish it. Haggai said "Be strong!" to the governor, the high priest, and the people working on the building, and those two words would be very significant to them.

During the Feast of Tabernacles, the Jews had the Book of Deuteronomy read to them (Deut. 31:9-13), so they heard the record of the three times Moses told Joshua and the people to be strong (Deut. 31:6-7, 23). No doubt they also remembered that three times the Lord told Joshua to be strong (Josh. 1:6-7, 9); and when King David charged Solomon with the task of building the original temple, three times he told his son to be strong (1 Chron. 22:13; 28:10, 20). "Be strong" wasn't an empty phrase; it was an important part of their own Jewish history.

It's one thing to tell people to be strong and work and quite something else to give them a solid foundation for those words of encouragement. Haggai told them why they should be strong and work, because the Lord was with them (Hag. 2:4; see 1:13).

The promise of God's presence was an encouragement to both Joshua (Josh. 1:5, 9; 3:7) and Solomon (1 Chron. 28:20). Believers today can claim the same promise as they serve the Lord, "For He Himself has said, 'I will never leave you nor forsake you'" (Heb. 13:5, NIV; and see Deut. 31:6, 8).

Encouragement: God's covenant (Hag. 2:5). The promise of God's presence with His people is guaranteed by His unchanging Word (v. 5). When the tabernacle was dedicated by Moses, God's presence moved in (Ex. 40:34-38), for the Lord had promised to dwell with His people. "Then I will dwell among the Israelites and be their God. They will know that I am the Lord their God, who brought them out of Egypt so that I might dwell among them" (Ex. 29:45-46, NIV). The same Holy Spirit who enabled Moses and the elders to lead the people (Num. 11:16-17, 25; Isa. 63:11) would enable the Jews to finish building the temple.

The Prophet Zechariah, who ministered with Haggai, also emphasized the importance of trusting the Holy Spirit for the enablement needed to do God's will: "Not by might, nor by power, but by my Spirit, saith the Lord of hosts" (Zech. 4:6). A.W. Tozer once said, "If God were to take the Holy Spirit out of this world, much of what we're doing in our churches would go right on, and nobody would know the difference." What an indictment!

Encouragement: God's promise (Hag. 2:6-7, 9). With prophetic insight, Haggai looked ahead to the time when the Son of God would minister in this temple and bring the glory of God into its precincts (John 1:14). Herod's temple replaced the temple Zerubbabel built, but the Jews still considered it "the second temple." Certainly the glory that Jesus brought into that temple was greater than the glory of the tabernacle or the temple Solomon built.

Then Haggai looked even farther into the future and saw the end of the ages, when God would shake the nations and Jesus would return (Hag. 2:7). This verse is quoted in Hebrews 12:26-27 and applied to the return of Christ at the end of the age. God had shaken Sinai when He gave the law (Heb. 12:18-21; Ex. 19:16-25), and He will shake the nations before He sends His Son (Matt. 24:29-30). But today, God's people belong to a kingdom which cannot be shaken (Heb. 12:28); and they will share the glory of Christ when He establishes that kingdom on earth.

In both Jewish and Christian tradition, the phrase "the desire of all nations" (Hag. 2:7) has been generally interpreted as a messianic title of Christ. The nations of the world inwardly desire what Christ alone can give, whether they recognize this spiritual yearning or not. Charles Wesley followed this interpretation when he wrote in his Christmas hymn "Hark! The Herald Angels Sing" —

> Come, Desire of nations, come!
> Fix in us Thy humble home . . .

In the Hebrew text, the verb "will come" is plural, while "desired" is singular; so some interpreters translate "desired" as a compound noun: "the desirable things of the nations," that is, their treasures. The remnant had no beautiful treasures with which to adorn their temple, but when

Messiah comes to reign, the treasures of the nations will be brought to Him and will be used for His glory.

The glory referred to in Haggai 2:7 is the glory that Jesus brought to the temple in Jerusalem, but the glory in verse 9 refers to the glory of the millennial temple that will function during Christ's reign on earth (Ezek. 40–48; see 43:1-12). Isaiah 60:1-5 and Zechariah 14:14 teach that the nations will bring their wealth to the King when Israel is established in the promised kingdom.

God not only promised the coming of Messiah and the glory of God in the future temples, but He also promised peace (Hag. 2:9). "In this place" refers to the city of Jerusalem where the Messiah will reign as "Prince of peace" (Isa. 9:6). Those who believe on Jesus today have peace with God (Rom. 5:1) because of His atoning death and victorious resurrection (Col. 1:20; John 20:19-21). They may also enjoy the "peace of God" as they yield to Christ and trust wholly in Him (Phil. 4:6-9).

Encouragement: God's provision (Hag. 2:8). Finally, the Lord assured them that, in spite of the bad economy and their lack of wealth, He was able to provide all they needed. "The silver is mine, and the gold is mine" (v. 8). True, the remnant had promises of provision from the government (Ezra 1:4; 3:7; 6:4), but government grants are limited. God owns all the wealth, even the wealth stored in the king's treasury, and He can distribute it as He desires. God promises to supply all our needs according to His riches in glory (Phil. 4:19).

It's better to fail in an endeavor that you know will ultimately succeed than to succeed in an endeavor you know will ultimately fail. The humble temple the Jewish remnant was constructing would not last, and even Herod's ornate temple would be destroyed by the Romans, but there would one day be a glorious temple that nobody could destroy or defile. Knowing this, the discouraged remnant could take courage and finish their work.

2. Looking within: contamination (Hag. 2:10-19)

About two months later (Dec. 18), the Lord spoke to Haggai again and gave him a message about sin. God couldn't bless the people the way He wanted to because they were defiled, so it was important that they keep themselves clean before the Lord. "Clean" and "unclean" were very important concepts to the Jews living under the Old Covenant; in fact, this is one of the major themes of the Book of Leviticus.[1] If a Jew became defiled, perhaps by touching a dead body or an open sore, he was separated from the rest of the camp and required to bathe before being allowed to return. In some instances, he had to offer a proper sacrifice to restore fellowship with the Lord.

Haggai went to the priests, who were the authorities on this subject, and asked them two simple questions, not for his own education (he certainly knew the law) but for the benefit of the people who were present.

Question #1—holiness (Hag. 2:11-12). When an animal was presented on the altar as a sacrifice, the meat was considered holy; that is, it belonged to the Lord and was set apart to be used only as He instructed. The priests and their families were permitted to eat portions of some of the sacrifices, but they had to be careful how they ate it, where they ate it, and what they did with the leftovers (Lev. 6:8–7:38).

"If a garment containing a piece of consecrated meat touches food," Haggai asked, "does the garment make the food holy?" The priests replied, "No." Why? Because you can't transmit holiness in such a simple manner. Even though the garment is holy (set apart) because of the sanctified meat, this holiness can't be imparted to other objects by the garment.[2]

Question #2—defilement (Hag. 2:13). "Suppose somebody touched a dead body and became unclean," Haggai said. "Could that person touch another person and make him unclean?" The answer was obviously, "Yes." Haggai had made his point: you can transmit defilement from one thing or person to another, but you can't transmit sanctity. The same principle applies in the area of health: you can transmit your sickness to healthy people and make them sick, but you can't share your health with them.

The application (vv. 14-19). "What is Haggai driving at?" the people no doubt were asking, so he told them. The people working on the temple couldn't impart any holiness to it, but they could defile it by their sins. Not only was it important that they do God's work, but it was also important that they do His work from hearts that were pure and devoted to God. The prophet reviewed their recent history. During the years when they were selfish, they experienced the discipline of the Lord (1:1-11). The Jews weren't keeping the terms of the covenant, so God couldn't bless them as He promised, and their economy fell apart. When the grain was in the fields, God smote it with mildew and hail, and after the grain had been harvested, the supply didn't last (Deut. 28:22).

Why had God done this to His people? To get them to turn back to Him with all their hearts. "Yet you did not turn to Me" (Hag. 2:17, NIV). They were so concerned to build their own houses that they ignored the house of God, and yet the rebuilding of the temple was the task that had brought them to Jerusalem!

Haggai was issuing a call to repentance, and with that call came the assurance of God's blessing (vv. 18-19). He was reminding the people of the promise God gave Solomon after the dedication of the temple: "If My people, who are called by My name, shall humble themselves, and pray, and seek My face, and turn from their wicked ways, then will I hear from heaven, and will forgive their sin, and will heal their land" (2 Chron. 7:14).

Had the workers been devoted to the Lord when the foundation of the temple was laid, God's blessing would have followed immediately; but the people were sinful at heart, and their sin grieved the Lord and defiled their work. "Is the seed yet in the barn?" he asked his congregation (Hag. 2:19); and they would have had to answer, "No." It was late December and the men had just plowed the fields for the winter crops. Haggai was calling on them to trust God for the future harvest. It was another example of Matthew 6:33: put God's interests first and He'll take care of the rest. "From this day will I bless you" (Hag. 2:19).

Many local church constitutions assign to the elders the "spiritual direction" of the church, and to the deacons the responsibilities for the "material" aspects of the ministry. For organizational purposes, this may be convenient, but this separation of "material" and "spiritual" is not biblical. The construction of a new church sanctuary should be just as spiritual an endeavor as an evangelistic crusade or a missions conference. One of the best ways to show our spiritual devotion to the Lord is by using material things to His glory, including money and buildings. The managing of material blessings demands as much sanctity as the managing of the "spiritual" ministries of the church.

It must always be that sin hinders the work of God and robs us of the blessings of God. It was the sins of the people that brought about the destruction of Jerusalem and the captivity of the nation, and their sins could hinder the rebuilding of the temple and the renewing of the Jewish nation in their own land. "Righteousness exalts a nation, but sin is a reproach to any people" (Prov. 14:34).

Haggai has asked the people to look back and then to look

within. They've learned about God's glory and God's holiness.

There is now a third look and a third lesson to learn.

3. Look ahead: coronation (Hag. 2:20-23)

Haggai has encouraged the Jewish people to stay on the job and finish God's house. Now he has a special word of encouragement for Zerubbabel the governor, and it was delivered on the same day as the third message, December 18. Being a faithful preacher of the Word, Haggai was always listening for God's voice and sensitive to whatever the Lord wanted him to say and do.

Zerubbabel was the grandson of King Jehoiachin (Jeconiah, Matt. 1:12; Coniah, Jer. 22:24, 28), and therefore of the royal line of David. But instead of wearing a crown and sitting on a throne, Zerubbabel was the humble governor of a struggling remnant of the Jewish nation, trying to complete the building of a rather inglorious temple. What a discouraging situation for a royal prince to be in!

So, God gave His servant Haggai a special word of encouragement for the governor. Were the nations around Jerusalem larger and stronger? Rest assured that the Lord will care for His people Israel as He has always done in the past. The same God who enabled Moses to defeat Egypt, and Joshua to conquer the nations in Canaan, would protect His people so that His purposes could be fulfilled through them. Israel will endure until the last days, and then the Lord will defeat her enemies and establish her in her kingdom.

The Lord called Zerubbabel "My servant," an exclusive title reserved for specially chosen people, and Zerubbabel was indeed chosen by the Lord. God compared him to a royal signet ring. The signet ring was used by kings to put their official "signature" on documents (Es. 3:10; 8:8, 10), the guarantee that the king would keep his promise and fulfill the terms of the document.

Zerubbabel's ancestor, King Jehoiachin (Coniah), had been rejected by God, but Zerubbabel was accepted by God. "'As I live,' says the Lord, 'though Coniah the son of Jehoiakim, king of Judah, were the signet on My right hand, yet would I pluck you off'" (Jer. 22:24, NKJV). God was reversing the judgment and renewing His promise that the Davidic line would not die out but would one day give the world a Savior. That's why we find Zerubbabel named in the genealogies of Jesus Christ (Matt. 1:12; Luke 3:27).

This message must have encouraged Zerubbabel to stay on the job and finish the work God gave him to do. He was special to God, chosen by God, the servant of God! He was as near and dear to God as a king's signet ring. The people of Israel would have many centuries of struggle and suffering before them, but the Messiah would come, and one day, Israel's enemies would be defeated and the glorious kingdom established.

As you read the Old Testament, you see how "salvation history" progressed from age to age, always moving toward the fulfillment of the messianic promise. Many people played different roles in the drama, but each of them was important. Abraham founded the nation, and Isaac and Jacob built it. Joseph protected it in Egypt and Moses redeemed the people from Egypt. Joshua gave them their promised inheritance, and David established the kingdom. In spite of sin, suffering, and failures, the Davidic line never ceased, and the day came when Jesus Christ, the Son of David, was born in Bethlehem.

When the Christian church celebrates the birth of Christ, people remember Mary and Joseph, the magi, the shepherds, and even wicked King Herod; but they rarely think about Zerubbabel, a humble player in the drama, but a faithful one.

We can't leave Haggai without noting some practical lessons for God's people today.

1. *The work of God is begun, sustained, and encouraged by the Word of God.* "So the elders of the Jews continued to build and prosper under the preaching of Haggai the prophet and Zechariah, a descendant of Iddo" (Ezra 6:14, NIV). When God's servants proclaim God's Word in the power of the Spirit, things begin to happen. "Is it not clear, as you take a bird's-eye view of church history," said Dr. D. Martyn Lloyd-Jones, "that the decadent periods and eras in the history of the church have always been those periods when preaching had declined? What is it that always heralds the dawn of a Reformation or of a revival? It is renewed preaching."[3]

2. *God's servants must work together to build God's temple.* Haggai and Zechariah, an older man and a younger man, both ministered the Word to the Jewish remnant, and God blessed their mutual efforts. It's tragic when preachers and churches compete with one another and even carry on public disputes that give the enemy ammunition to oppose the Gospel. "For we are laborers together with God" (1 Cor. 3:9).

3. *When the outlook is bleak, try the uplook.* Apart from God's promises, we have no hope. As Vance Havner used to say, "Faith sees the invisible, chooses the imperishable, and does the impossible." Our work today is a part of God's work in the future, and we want to do our best.

4. *Putting God first is the guarantee of God's best blessing.* Why should God's work suffer while we pursue pleasure and comfort for ourselves? An affluent generation of Christians that is wasting God's generous gifts on trivia and toys will have much to answer for when the Lord returns. Matthew 6:33 is still in the Bible, and so is Romans 14:12.

5. *Apart from the power of the Holy Spirit, our labors are in vain.* "For it is God who works in you both to will and to do

for His good pleasure" (Phil. 2:13, NKJV). God still demon-
strates His power and receives great glory through the weak
things of this world (1 Cor. 1:26-31). If we're too strong in
ourselves, the Lord can't use us. That's what ruined King
Uzziah; "for he was greatly helped until he became powerful"
(2 Chron. 26:15).

Now, we turn to Haggai's associate, the young prophet
Zechariah, and study his striking prophecies and Jerusalem,
the Jews and the Messiah.

Zechariah in His Time

Thirty-one men in the Bible have the name Zechariah, which means "the Lord remembers." (See Zech. 10:9 and Luke 1:72.) The Prophet Zechariah was a young man when he wrote this book (Zech. 2:4), so he must have been born in Babylon and come to Judah with Zerubbabel in 537.

His father, Berechiah, probably died young, and his grandfather Iddo adopted him and raised him (Zech. 1:1; Ezra 6:14). Iddo was a priest (Neh. 12:1-4, 16), so Zechariah was both a prophet and a priest, like Ezekiel and John the Baptist.[1] He began to preach about two months after Haggai began his ministry (Hag. 1:1) and a little over a month after the Jews resumed the work of rebuilding their temple (Hag. 1:15; Ezra 5:2).

Haggai's ministry was aimed at arousing the Jews to action, while Zechariah's messages were given for their encouragement (Zech. 1:13). Both prophets motivated the people by predicting future glory for the temple and future greatness for Israel. Zechariah has much to say about the future of Jerusalem and the coming of Messiah. He presents Messiah as a king (9:9), a stone (3:9; 10:4), a slave sold for thirty pieces of silver (11:12), the smitten shepherd (13:7), the Branch (3:8; 6:12), and the glorious Redeemer and Ruler of Israel (14:1-4, 9, 16-17).

We know nothing about Zechariah's life or death. His prophecy is quoted or alluded to at least forty-one times in the New Testament.

A Suggested Outline of the Book of Zechariah

Key Theme: God's jealous concern for Jerusalem and the Jews

Key verse: Zechariah 1:14

I. God calls His people to repent —1:1-6

II. God encourages His people to trust Him—1:7–6:15

    1. Eight night visions

        (1) The horsemen: God watches the nations—1:7-17

        (2) The horns and smiths: the nations judged—1:18-21

        (3) The measuring line: Jerusalem restored—2:1-13

        (4) The high priest: Israel cleansed—3:1-10

        (5) The olive trees: God empowers His people—4:1-14

        (6) The flying scroll: evil purged from the land—5:1-4

        (7) The ephah: evil taken to Babylon—5:5-11

        (8) The four chariots: the Gentiles judged—6:1-8

    2. The crowning of Joshua: Messiah will reign—6:9-15

III. God instructs His people—7:1–8:23

      1. About true fasting—7:1-7

      2. About obedience to the Word—7:8-14

      3. About Jerusalem's future—8:1-23

IV. God redeems His people—9:1–14:21

    Two oracles

      1. The rejection of Messiah—9:1–11:17

      2. The return and reign of Messiah—12:1–14:21

The messages in chapters 1–8 were given to Zechariah during the building of the temple, and those in chapters 9–14 after the temple was completed.

God and His People

A young preacher in his first pastorate phoned me for encouragement "Most of the people in the church are older than I am," he said. "I wonder if they pay any attention to me. I feel like I'm out of place preaching to them."

Since I had faced the same situation in my first church, I was able to give him the same answer a veteran pastor gave me when I asked for help. "As long as you're delivering God's message, don't worry about how old you are. When you open that Bible, you're over 2,000 years old!"

Zechariah was a young man (Zech. 2:4) when God called him to minister to the struggling Jewish remnant trying to rebuild their temple in the ruined city of Jerusalem. The elder Prophet Haggai had delivered two of his messages before Zechariah joined him in ministry, and the two of them served God together for a short time. Haggai had gotten the building program going again after a sixteen-year hiatus, and now Zechariah would encourage the people to finish their work. God gave the young man "good and comforting words" (1:13, 17) to assure the people that, in spite of the hard times, God was with them and would see them through.

The prophet had two major emphases as he began his ministry to the remnant: God was calling them to repent, and God was assuring them of His personal concern. In a series of eight night visions, God explained His involvement with His people.

1. God calls His people to repent (Zech. 1:1-6)

A preacher's first sermon is usually difficult to deliver, but in Zechariah's case, his first message was doubly difficult because of the theme—repentance. God commanded His young servant to call the discouraged remnant to turn from their wicked ways and obey His Word. Zechariah boldly proclaimed what God told him to say, for, after all, the Lord couldn't bless His chosen people until they were clean in His sight. If Zechariah had wanted to quote a text for his sermon, it could well have been 2 Chronicles 7:14, a verse the Jewish people knew well.

Zechariah invited the people to look back and recall what their forefathers had done to provoke the Lord to anger and judgment (Zech. 1:2, 4). The Jewish people who had returned to the land knew their nation's history very well. They knew that God had sent prophet after prophet to plead with their forefathers to turn from idolatry and return to the Lord, but the nation had refused to listen.

Isaiah had warned the leaders that God would discipline the nation if they didn't change their ways (Isa. 2:6–3:26; 5:1-30; 29:1-14). Jeremiah wept as he warned Judah and Jerusalem that judgment was coming from the north (Babylon) and that the Jews would be exiled for seventy years (Jer. 1:13-16; 4:5-9; 6:22-26; 25:1-14). "And the Lord God of their fathers sent warnings to them by His messengers, rising up early and sending them, because He had compassion on His people and on His dwelling place. But they mocked the messengers of God, despised His words, and scoffed at His prophets, until the wrath of the Lord arose against His people, till there was no remedy" (2 Chron. 36:15-16, NKJV).

Then, Zechariah *shared God's promise with them:* "Return to Me...and I will return to you" (Zech. 1:3, NIV). God had left His people to their own ways, and that was why they were experiencing so much trouble. Haggai had already told them this in his first message (Hag. 1), but it was worth repeating. "Draw near to God and He will draw near to you" (James 4:8, NKJV). A.W. Tozer reminds us that "nearness is likeness,"[2] so, if we want to be close to God, we must be obedient and develop godly character. The remnant had not put God first, so He couldn't bless them as He desired to do.

At this point, Zechariah *asked them two questions:* "Your fathers, where are they? And the prophets, do they live forever?" (Zech. 1:5) Had the listeners answered honestly, they would have said, "Many of our fathers are dead because they were slain by the Babylonians, and some are still in exile in Babylon. Some of the prophets are dead because our ancestors killed them."

But the point Zechariah was making was that the death of the prophets indicated the loss of opportunity for the nation. God gave the Jews ample time to repent and escape punishment, but they wasted their opportunity, and now it was too late. However, the Word of God, spoken and written by the prophets, can never die, and that Word eventually "catches up with" rebellious sinners (v. 6; "take hold of"; "overtake," NIV). Once God's long-suffering runs out, His living words will track down the offenders and judge them.[3]

Some of their forefathers did repent (v. 6), but their repentance came too late to prevent the destruction of Jerusalem and the deportation of the people. Some Jews may have repented when Nebuchadnezzar and his army arrived at the gates of Jerusalem, while others turned to God while exiled in Babylon. They admitted that their punishment was deserved and that God was just (see Lam. 2:17).

By calling the people to repent, Zechariah was preparing them for the messages he would give them, for unless our hearts are right with God, we can't hear His Word with true spiritual comprehension. "Today, if you will hear His voice, do not harden your hearts" (Heb. 3:7, NKJV).

We occasionally hear evangelists calling lost sinners to repent, and this is good and biblical. But we rarely hear preachers calling God's people to repent, even though this was the message of the prophets, John the Baptist, and Jesus. "The last word of our Lord to the church is not the Great Commission," said Vance Havner. "The Great Commission is indeed our program to the end of the age, but our Lord's last word to the church is 'Repent.'" [4] It's one thing to ask God to bless us but quite another to be the kind of people He can bless!

2. God comforts His people (Zech. 1:7-17)

About three months later, during the night of February 15, 519, Zechariah had a series of eight visions that God gave to encourage the remnant and motivate them to finish rebuilding the temple. These visions focus primarily on God's ministry to Israel and His judgment on the Gentile nations that have afflicted Israel.

The army (vv. 7-11). In the first vision, the prophet saw a man on a red (bay) horse, leading an army astride red, brown, and white horses. This "man among the myrtle trees" was the Angel of the Lord (vv. 11-13), the second Person of the Godhead, who in Old Testament times made temporary preincarnate appearances on earth. As the Angel of the Lord, the Son of God appeared to Hagar (Gen. 16:7-14), Abraham (18; 22:11-18), Jacob (31:11, 13), Moses (Ex. 3), Gideon (Jud. 6:11-23), and Samson's parents (Jud. 13).

But there was also an "interpreting angel" there who explained various things to Zechariah (Zech. 1:9, 13-14, 19; 2:3; 4:1, 4-5; 5:10; 6:4-5). Ten times during these visions, Zechariah asked questions of this angel and received replies (1:9, 19, 21; 2:2; 4:4, 11-12; 5:5, 10; 6:6). "If any of you lacks wisdom, let him ask of God, who gives to all liberally and without reproach, and it will be given to him" (James 1:5, NKJV). "The secret of the Lord is with those who fear Him, and He will show them His covenant" (Ps. 25:14).

In this first vision, the Angel of the Lord taught Zechariah the meaning of the horsemen (Zech. 1:10): they are God's angelic army that patrols the earth and carries out the decrees of the Lord (v. 11, and see Deut. 33:2; 1 Kings 22:19; Job 1:6-7; 2:1-2; Dan. 7:10; Matt. 27:63). Jehovah is "Lord of Hosts," the Commander of the armies of heaven and earth.

The messengers reported that the Gentile nations were "at rest and in peace." After the upheaval of empires and Persia's conquest of Babylon and other nations, this would appear to be an encouraging report, but it really wasn't. The Jewish remnant was in distress while the Gentile powers were at ease. Haggai had promised that the Lord would shake the nations and redeem His people (Hag. 2:6-9, 20-23), but this important event hadn't occurred yet. The kingdom promised by the prophets seemed to be a dream that would never come true.

The appeal (Zech. 1:12). A remarkable thing happened: the Son of God interceded for the people of God who were in great affliction! For centuries, "How long?" has been the cry of suffering people, especially the people of Israel (Pss. 74:9-10; 79:5; 80:4; 89:46; Hab. 1:2). "How long?" is even the cry of the martyred saints in heaven (Rev. 6:10). That the Son of God should so identify Himself with the cries of His people reveals His compassion and concern. "In all their distress he too was distressed" (Isa. 63:9, NIV).

Jeremiah had promised that God's blessing would come after the seventy years of captivity (Jer. 25:8-14; 29:10-11), but the nation was still suffering.[5] Why? Because they forgot that God had attached conditions to that blessing: the people had to repent, call upon God, and seek Him with all their heart, the very thing Zechariah had preached. Intercession for Israel should still be a part of our prayers. Moses (Ex. 32; Deut. 9:18), the prophets (1 Sam. 12:23; 1 Kings 18; Jer. 9:1; Hab. 3), Jesus (Luke 23:34), and Paul (Rom. 10:1) all prayed for Israel; good examples for us to follow. "You who call on the Lord, give yourselves no rest, and give Him no rest till He establishes Jerusalem and makes her the praise of the earth" (Isa. 62:6-7). "Pray for the peace of Jerusalem; they shall prosper who love thee" (Ps. 122:6).

The answer (Zech. 1:13-17). After interceding for Israel, the Lord gave "comforting words" to the angel to give to the prophet.[6] He affirmed His jealous love and concern for Jerusalem (see 8:2). God is jealous over His chosen people as a husband is jealous over his wife and as parents over their children (Ex. 20:5; Deut. 4:24; 5:9; 6:15). This explains why the Lord accused the Jews of adultery and unfaithfulness whenever they were guilty of worshiping heathen gods (Jer. 2:1-3; 3:14; 31:32; Hosea 1). Worldliness on the part of Christians is also pictured as "spiritual adultery" (James 4:4-10).

The Lord was angry with the Gentile nations because they had been unnecessarily brutal toward the Jews. True, God had called Assyria to punish the Northern Kingdom of Israel, and Babylon to chasten Judah; but these nations went beyond what God called them to do and tried to destroy the Jews. Other nations, like Moab, had also joined in the assault (see Pss. 83 and 137).

But the Lord's most heartening words had to do with Judah's future, not her enemies, for God promised to return to His people and prosper their nation. He would comfort Zion and prove to the enemy nations that Jerusalem was indeed His chosen city. This promise is repeated and expanded in the rest of Zechariah's prophecy.

When our situation appears to be hopeless, we must remind ourselves that God identifies with our sufferings and is in charge of the future. Our responsibility is to repent, confess our sins, and believe His "comforting words." His responsibility is to respond to our faith and work out His perfect will for us.

3. God vindicates His people (Zech. 1:18-21)

Over the centuries, the Jews have suffered repeatedly at the hands of many nations, and yet they have survived. But every nation that has sought to destroy the Jews has discovered the truth of God's promise to Abraham, "I will bless those who bless you, and I will curse him who curses you" (Gen. 12:3).

That's the message of the second vision that God gave to Zechariah: the nations that have scattered the Jews will be terrified and thrown down by God's agents of judgment. In a letter to President Ronald Reagan, Israeli Prime Minister Menachem Begin wrote, "My generation, dear Ron, swore on the altar of God that whoever proclaims the intent of destroying the Jewish state or the Jewish people, or both, seals his fate."[7] But it's the Lord who does the judging, not the armies of Israel, and His judgments are never wrong.

In Scripture, a horn is a symbol of power, especially the power of a nation or a ruler (Pss. 75:4-5; 89:17; 92:10; Jer. 48:25; Amos 6:13; Dan. 7:7-12; 8:1ff; Rev. 17). The four "smiths" (artisans, craftsmen) represent nations that God uses to defeat the enemies of the Jews. They would use their "tools" to cut off the horns and render them powerless.

The concept of four horns (nations) reminds us of

Daniel's visions of the image (Dan. 2) and the beasts (Dan. 7), both of which speak of four empires: Babylon, Medo-Persia, Greece, and Rome.[8] In 722, Assyria devastated the Northern Kingdom of Israel, but God raised up Babylon to defeat Assyria (Jer. 25:9; 27:6) and eventually take Judah into captivity in 586. Babylon did indeed oppress the Jews, but then God raised up Cyrus to conquer Babylon in 539 (Isa. 44:28; 45:1); and in 538, he permitted the Jews to return to their land. The Persians were conquered by the Greeks, under Alexander the Great,[9] and Greece was conquered by Rome.

This scenario suggests that the "horns" also became "smiths" as each empire conquered the previous oppressors. It also reminds the Jews of God's providential care in the past and His promise of protection for the future, *for God will not permit any nation to annihilate His chosen people.* In the last days, when Antichrist, the "dreadful and terrible beast," establishes his kingdom (Dan. 7:7-8, 15-28) and persecutes the Jews, he and his kingdom will be destroyed by the return of Jesus Christ in glory and power. Zechariah will have more to say about this in the last part of his book.

4. God will restore His people (Zech. 2:1-13)

The remnant that had returned to Judah was concerned about rebuilding the temple and restoring the city and the nation, but their work was extremely difficult. In this vision, God assured His people that He planned future glory and honor for them and their city when He Himself would come to dwell with them.

Anticipation (vv. 1-3). If a total stranger came into my house and began to measure the windows for curtains and the floor for carpeting, I'd probably ask him to leave. After all, you measure property that belongs to you, over which you have authority. When the prophet saw a man measuring

Jerusalem, it was evidence that Jerusalem was God's city and that one day He would claim it and restore it in glory.

The man with the measuring line is evidently the Angel of the Lord, Israel's Messiah. Leaders and diplomats may debate over who shall control Jerusalem, but the Lord Jesus Christ has the final word. By measuring the city, He declares that it is His and He will accomplish His divine purposes for the city no matter what leaders and international assemblies may decide.

But this symbolic act declares something else: Jerusalem will enjoy future expansion and glory such as the city has never experienced. The population will spill over the walls; in fact, there will be no need of walls because God will be a "wall of fire" around His people. (See Isa. 49:13-21 and 54:1-3.) The small remnant of Jews in ruined Jerusalem were helping to keep alive a city that would one day be greatly honored and blessed by Almighty God!

Admonition (Zech. 2:6-9). The Lord admonished the Jews yet in Babylon to leave the city and join the remnant in Jerusalem. Why remain in the comfort and security of a pagan society when they were desperately needed in their own land? The day would come when Babylon, now under Persian rule, would be judged for her sins and those who served her would plunder her. Get out while there is still opportunity!

This admonition didn't imply that every Jew who remained in Babylon was out of the will of God. Just as God sent Joseph to Egypt to prepare the way for his family, so He had people like Esther and Mordecai, Daniel and his friends, and Nehemiah, in places of authority in pagan cities where they could do the work He planned for them to do. The Lord was summoning the Jews who were putting comfort, vocation, and security ahead of doing God's work in their own sacred city. (See Isa. 48:20 and 52:11; Jer. 50:8 and 51:6, 9, 45;

2 Cor. 6:14-18; and Rev. 18:4.)

The Jews are very precious to God; He called them "the apple [pupil] of His eye" (Zech. 2:8; Deut. 32:10; Ps. 17:8). The pupil is the tiny opening in the iris that lets in the light, and this is a very delicate and important area of that vital organ. Hence, anything dear and precious is like the pupil of the eye.[10]

Messiah is still speaking when He says, "He [God the Father] sent Me after glory" (Zech. 2:8, NKJV), that is, "to bring Him glory." The whole purpose of Christ's life on earth, His ministry, and His death and resurrection was to bring glory to God (John 1:14; 12:23, 28; 17:4); and part of that glory will involve the future restoration of Israel in the kingdom when He reigns on earth (Isa. 61:3-11).

Acclamation (Zech. 2:10-13). Promises like these ought to make God's people "sing and rejoice" ("shout and be glad," NIV). Their Messiah will come and dwell with them, just as the glory of God had dwelt in the tabernacle and the temple. Ezekiel describes the new city and temple in Ezekiel 40–48, and closes his book by naming the glorious new city "Jehovah Shammah," which means "the Lord is there" (48:35). In that day, many Gentiles will trust in the Lord and be joined with Israel in the glorious kingdom over which Messiah will reign (Isa. 2:1-5; 19:23-25; 60:1-3; Zech. 8:20-23).

Zechariah 2:12 is the only place in Scripture where Palestine is called "the holy land." That designation is often used today, but it really doesn't apply. The land will not be holy until Messiah cleanses the people and the land when He returns to reign (3:9). A fountain will be opened to wash away sin and uncleanness (13:1), and then the Jews shall be called "the holy people" (Isa. 62:12). That's something to shout about!

But it's also something to make the nations of the world pause and consider in awesome silence (Zech. 2:13; Hab.

2:20; Zeph. 1:7). Why? Because before Messiah comes to reign, He will judge the nations of the earth during that period of time called "the time of Jacob's trouble" (Jer. 30:7), "the day of the Lord" (Isa. 2:12; 13:6, 9; Joel 1:15; 2:1ff; Zech. 14:1), and "the great tribulation" (Matt. 24:21; Rev. 6–19). It will be a time of intense suffering when the nations will receive their just sentence for their inhumanity and ungodliness. When the Lord has "roused Himself from His holy dwelling" (Zech. 2:13, NIV), the nations of the world will experience divine wrath; and there will be no escape.

As you review these three night visions, you learn that God watches the nations and knows what they are doing; that He judges the nations for their sins, especially for their mistreatment of Israel; and that there is a glorious future planned for Jerusalem and the Jewish nation, when Messiah will return to cleanse them and restore the glory of God in their midst.

No wonder we're taught to pray, "Thy kingdom come" (Matt. 6:10); for when we pray that prayer, we are praying for the peace of Jerusalem. And there can be no true peace in Jerusalem until the Prince of Peace reigns in glory.

EIGHT

God and His Leaders

According to management experts James M. Kouzes and Barry Z. Posner, one of the popular myths about leadership is that "leaders are prescient visionaries with Merlin-like powers."[1] In other words, leaders know everything and can do anything. But if that were true, leadership wouldn't be the difficult and demanding task that it is. Certainly successful leaders enjoy the "peaks" and "perks" that go with their positions, but they also have to deal with the valleys and sacrifices that are also a big part of the job. Real leadership isn't easy.

Zechariah 3 and 4 focus on Joshua and Zerubbabel, the two leaders of the Jewish remnant who knew how tough it is to lead. Joshua was high priest and had the concern for the spiritual life of the people, while Zerubbabel was governor and had the responsibility of managing the civil affairs of the nation. But their work wasn't easy. Zerubbabel was trying to motivate people who were discouraged and selfish, and Joshua was trying to educate people who were disobedient and sinful. Is there any hope for a defiled and discouraged nation, or a defiled and discouraged church or individual?

Yes, there is! God gave the Prophet Zechariah two visions that speak to us today and encourage us to keep serving the

Lord no matter how difficult the people or circumstances may be.

1. God cleanses His people for service (Zech. 3:1-10)

Haggai's first message (Hag. 1:1-11) and Zechariah's call to repentance (Zech. 1:1-6) are evidence that the spiritual level of the Jewish remnant was very low.[2] Most of these people had been born in Babylon, where there wasn't much religious example or instruction to nourish their worship of Jehovah; and the difficult circumstances in their own land tested their faith greatly.

The accused (3:1a, 3). Joshua stood before the Lord as a representative of Israel, a people He had called to be a holy nation of priests (Ex. 19:5-6). He wore filthy clothes, not because he was sinful personally, but because the people had sinned and were unclean in God's sight. The emphasis here is on the nation collectively and not on Joshua individually, for both Joshua and Zerubbabel were "men symbolic of things to come" (v. 8, NIV). God had chosen Jerusalem and had plucked the Jews out of the fire of Babylonian Captivity (v. 2). What God did for Joshua symbolically He would do for Israel personally: the iniquity of the land would be removed in a day (v. 9).

To "stand before the Lord" means to be in a place of service (Gen. 41:46; Deut. 10:8; 1 Sam. 16:21), so the Jews became defiled while they were attempting to serve the Lord. If *their service* was unclean in God's sight, what must *their deliberate sins* have been like! The Hebrew word translated "filthy" denotes the worst kind of defilement possible for a Jew. According to Merrill Unger, the word can be translated "excrement-covered."[3]

Since the priests were commanded to keep themselves clean at all times, on penalty of death (Ex. 28:39-43; 30:17-21), Joshua's wearing filthy garments would be a terrible personal embarrassment and an offense against God's law. Those garments were "for glory and for beauty" (Ex. 28:2, 40), but the Lord saw neither glory nor beauty as He beheld His servant.

The accuser (Zech. 3:1b). Zechariah has described a courtroom scene, in which Joshua is the defendant, God is the Judge, Satan is the prosecuting attorney, and Jesus Christ is the defense attorney, the Advocate of God's people before the holy throne of God (1 John 2:1-2). The word "Satan" means "adversary" and refers to the enemy who resists God's work and God's people. Satan has access to the throne of God (Job 1–2) where he accuses God's people (Rev. 12:10). When Satan talks to us about God, he lies, but when he talks to God about us, he tells the truth!

God's throne is a throne of justice and God is a righteous Judge. Knowing this, Satan pointed out Joshua's defilement, which symbolized the defilement of the nation, and insisted that a holy God punish His sinful people. It seemed like an airtight case, except for one factor: the grace of God.

The Advocate (Zech. 3:2-5). Christ's present ministry in heaven is twofold. He's our High Priest, interceding for us and giving us the grace we need for life and service here on earth (Heb. 4:14-16; 13:20-21); and He's our Advocate, representing us before the throne of God when we do sin (1 John 2:1-2). Don't get the erroneous idea that the Father yearns to punish us and the Son pleads with Him to change His mind, because that isn't the picture at all. The Father and the Son both love us and want the best for us, but God can't ignore our sins and still be a holy God.

This explains why Jesus took His wounds back to heaven with Him (Luke 24:39-40; John 20:20, 25-27): they prove that He was "delivered over to death for our sins and was raised to life for our justification" (Rom. 3:25, NIV). *Satan cannot accuse us, nor God condemn us, for sins for which Christ died!* "There is therefore now no condemnation to them which are in Christ Jesus" (Rom. 8:1).

The Lord rebuked Satan on the basis of His own electing grace: He had chosen Jerusalem and the Jewish nation in His own love and grace (Deut. 7:7-11; Pss. 33:12; 132:13). He had not chosen them because of their good works, so how could He condemn them for their bad works? "Who shall bring a charge against God's elect? It is God who justifies. Who is he who condemns? It is Christ who died, and furthermore is also risen, who is even at the right hand of God, who also makes intercession for us" (Rom. 8:33-34, NKJV).

God proved His grace to Israel by rescuing them from Babylonian Captivity; the Jews were "a brand plucked out of the fire" (Zech. 3:2; see Amos 4:11). Scripture often compares Israel's sufferings to going through the fire. Their trials in Egypt were like being in a furnace (Deut. 4:20), and the exile in Babylon was compared to being refined in the fire (Isa. 48:10; see 43:1-6). When Israel goes through the Tribulation in the end times, it will be an experience of refining (Zech. 13:9; Jer. 30:7).

The answer (Zech. 3:4-5). The same Savior who died for our sins arose from the dead and now intercedes for His people at the throne of God (Heb. 7:23-28). "If we confess our sins, He is faithful and just to forgive us our sins, and to cleanse us from all unrighteousness" (1 John 1:9). God's reply to Satan's accusation was to say to the angels before His throne, "Take away the filthy garments from him." This is forgiveness.

He gave a word of assurance to Joshua: "See, I have taken away your sin" (Zech. 3:4, NIV). Believers today know they are forgiven when they confess their sins, because they have the assurance of His promise. According to 1 John 1:9, God is not only faithful [to His promise], but He is also just [toward His Son] and will not condemn His people for sins for which His own Son had already been condemned.

But God in His grace goes beyond forgiveness and clothes

us in His own righteousness. "I will put rich garments on you" (Zech. 3:4, NIV). Adam and Eve tried to hide their guilt under garments of their own making (Gen. 3:7), but God killed animals and clothed them in skins (v. 21). Blood was shed that sin might be forgiven. "I will greatly rejoice in the Lord, my soul shall be joyful in my God; for He has clothed me with the garments of salvation, He has covered me with the robe of righteousness" (Isa. 61:10, NKJV; see Luke 15:22).

The climax of the cleansing (forgiveness) and robing (righteous in Christ, 2 Cor. 5:21) was the placing of the special turban on Joshua's head; for the golden plate at the front of the turban was inscribed: HOLINESS TO THE LORD (Ex. 28:36-38; 39:30-31). It was this that made him, the people, and their gifts acceptable to the Lord. We have no righteousness of our own, but we come in the righteousness and merits of Jesus Christ, our Savior (1 Peter 2:5).

The assurance (Zech. 3:6-7). The Lord Jesus Christ gave a charge to Joshua, because cleansing and restoration always involve responsibility. Joshua and his fellow priests weren't put on probation; they were cleansed and restored to service. But the continuation of their service depended on their faithfulness to the Lord and His Word. It's a privilege to serve the Lord, and we must never take it for granted.

"I will give you a place among these standing here" (v. 6, NIV) indicates that Joshua's service was in cooperation with the angels of God! (See v. 4, "those who stood before him.") The angels are God's servants, obeying His every command without fail, and God's earthly servants are united with them in accomplishing His will. "Your will be done on earth as it is in heaven" (Matt. 6:10, NKJV). God's invisible messengers play a vital part in His plans both for Israel (Dan. 10:10-21; Matt. 24:31) and the church (Heb. 1:13-14).

The announcement (Zech. 3:8-10). This remarkable announcement to Joshua and his fellow priests focuses on

Jesus Christ and presents three different images of the coming Messiah: the Priest, the Branch, and the Stone. Zechariah will say more about the priest in 6:9-15, so we'll save our detailed study for that passage. In their priestly ministry, Joshua and his associates were "symbolic of things to come" (3:8, NIV).

"The Branch" is an image of Messiah frequently found in the prophets (Isa. 11:1-2). Here Messiah is called "my servant the Branch." He is also "the Branch of the Lord" (4:2), "the Branch of righteousness" raised up for David (Jer. 23:5; 33:15), and "the man whose name is the Branch" (Zech. 6:12-13). These four titles parallel four aspects of the person of Christ as seen in the four Gospels:

Branch of righteousness for David—
Matthew, Gospel of the King

My servant the Branch—Mark, Gospel of the Servant

The man whose name is the Branch—
Luke, Gospel of the Son of Man

The Branch of the Lord—John, Gospel of the Son of God

"The stone" is another image of Messiah found often in Scripture, revealing several aspects of His ministry. Messiah is the cornerstone (Ps. 118:22-23; Matt. 21:42; Eph. 2:19-22; 1 Peter 2:7; see Zech. 10:4, NIV), a stone of stumbling (Isa. 8:14; 1 Peter 2:8; Rom. 9:32-33), the rejected stone (Ps. 118:22-23; Matt. 21:42), the smitten stone (Ex. 17:6; 1 Cor. 10:4), and the smiting stone (Dan. 2:34-35). At His first advent, Jesus was a stumbling stone to Israel who rejected Him, but He became the foundation stone for the church. At His second advent, He will smite the kingdoms of the world and establish His glorious kingdom.

The seven "eyes" on the stone probably speak of our

Lord's omniscience (Zech. 4:10, NIV; Rev. 5:6). The NIV margin translates it "seven facets," making this stone a precious and beautiful jewel because of the way it is engraved (cut). But the text refers to an inscription that God engraved on the stone, not a jewel, and it doesn't tell us what the inscription says. Some of the Church Fathers interpreted this engraving to mean the glorified wounds on Christ's body, but we have no indication from the text that this interpretation is warranted.

The key message of this difficult verse is the removal of Israel's sins in one day. This miracle of grace is described in Zechariah 5 and 12:10–13:1, and will be considered in later chapters. At the Second Advent, when Israel beholds the One whom they pierced (12:10), they will repent and be cleansed. "Who has ever heard of such a thing? Who has ever seen such things? Can a country be born in a day or a nation be brought forth in a moment?" (Isa. 66:8)

When that happens, God will fulfill the promises of peace that He has made to Israel through the prophets. Resting under one's vine and fig tree (Zech. 3:10) is an image of peace and security (1 Kings 4:25; 2 Kings 18:31; Micah 4:4), something that Israel has always longed for but has never found.

Knowing that God would forgive and cleanse His people and restore the ministry of His priests must have encouraged Joshua greatly. In the next vision, God will encourage His servant Zerubbabel.

2. God empowers His people for service (Zech. 4:1-14)
The young prophet had seen four wonderful visions, and the experience had exhausted him. He fell asleep and had to be awakened by the "interpreting angel" before God could reveal the fifth vision to him. Seeing divine visions and understanding their meanings made Daniel very weary and like a man who was dumb and without strength (Dan. 10:8, 15-19).

The flippant jovial manner in which some of God's people speak of prophetic matters today makes us wonder if they have really seen what the Word of God communicates about the future.

The vision (Zech. 4:1-3, 11-14). In the holy place of the tabernacle, in front of the veil and to the left of the altar of incense, stood a golden candlestick with seven branches (Ex. 25:31-40).[4] At the end of each branch was a golden lamp, and it was the high priest's duty each morning and evening to trim the wicks and provide the oil needed to keep the lamp burning (Lev. 24:3). This candlestick provided light in the holy place so the priests could see to burn the incense on the golden altar each morning and evening (Ex. 30:7-8).

But the candlestick that Zechariah saw was totally unlike the one Moses had put into the tabernacle. Along with the seven branches and lamps, this candlestick had a bowl at the top into which olive oil dripped from two olive trees (Zech. 4:3), which symbolized Joshua and Zerubbabel (v. 14). The candlestick also had seven pipes going from the bowl to each lamp, making a total of forty-nine pipes. No priest had to provide the oil because it was always coming from the trees. Seven pipes to each lamp assured an ample supply of fuel to keep the lights burning.

The lampstand in the tabernacle was symbolic of Messiah, the light of the world (John 8:12), who one day would come and give the "light of life" to all who would trust Him. The light from the golden lampstand would shine on the table in the holy place (Ex. 26:35) and reveal the loaves of bread, Christ the bread of life (Ex. 25:30; John 6:33, 35, 48, 50-51).

The tabernacle candlestick also spoke of the nation of Israel, the nation God had chosen to be a light in a spiritually dark world (Isa. 60:1-3; 62:1). (The seven-branched candlestick, the menorah, is the official symbol of the modern State of Israel.) The light was burning very low when the remnant returned to the land to rebuild the temple, and Zerubbabel wasn't sure there was enough power to keep the work going.

Believers today must keep in mind that the church is a light in a dark world, and we must depend on the Holy Spirit to enable us to bear witness (Matt. 5:14-16; Phil. 2:14-16). In Revelation 1–3, local churches are symbolized by individual lampstands, and the purpose of a lampstand is to give light. If we don't do what Christ commands us to do, He may take away the lampstand (2:5).

God provides the power (Zech. 4:4-7a). When Solomon built the temple which the Babylonians destroyed, he had almost unlimited resources at his disposal. His father David had fought many battles and collected spoil to be used in building the temple (1 Chron. 26:20, 27-28), but the remnant didn't have an army. Solomon was monarch of a powerful kingdom that ruled over many Gentile nations and took tribute from them, but the Jews in Zechariah's day had no such authority.

That's why God said to them through His prophet, "Not by might nor by power, but by My Spirit" (Zech. 4:6). The word "might" refers to military might, what people can do together, but the remnant had no army. "Power" refers to the strength of the individual, but Zerubbabel's strength was no doubt waning. "Don't be discouraged!" was the prophet's message. "The Spirit of God will enable us to do what an army could never do!" Had they forgotten what Haggai said to them? "My Spirit remains among you. Do not fear" (Hag. 2:5, NIV).

There are three ways we can attempt to do the work of God: we can trust our own strength and wisdom; we can borrow the resources of the world; or we can depend on the power of God. The first two approaches may appear to succeed, but they'll fail in the end. Only work done through the power of the Spirit will glorify God and endure the fires of His judgment (1 Cor. 3:12-15).

With their limited resources, completing the temple must

have looked to those Jews as impossible as moving a mountain, but God told Zerubbabel that he would, by God's power, level the mountain and make it a plain! Jesus told His disciples that exercising faith like a mustard seed (small but alive) could move mountains (Matt. 17:20; 21:21).

What "mountains" was Zerubbabel facing? Discouragement among the people, opposition from the enemies around them, poor crops, an unstable economy, people not obeying God's Law—problems not too different from those the people of God have faced throughout the centuries. The answer to these problems is *prayer that releases the Holy Spirit's power.* When the early Christians faced problems, they turned to God in prayer, and He answered by giving them a fresh filling of the Holy Spirit (Acts 4:23-31).

"We say we depend on the Holy Spirit," wrote Vance Havner, "but actually we are so wired up with our own devices that if the fire does not fall from heaven, we can turn on a switch and produce false fire of our own. If there is no sound of a rushing mighty wind, we have the furnace all set to blow hot air instead. God save us from a synthetic Pentecost!"[5]

God finishes His work (Zech. 4:7b-10). God assured Zerubbabel that he would complete the rebuilding of the temple and the people would rejoice at what God had done through them. Zerubbabel would "bring out the capstone [the last stone to be placed in the building] with shouts of 'God bless it! God bless it!'" (v. 7b, NIV) Another possible translation is "Beauty! Perfection!" That wasn't what some of the people were saying when the foundation of the temple was laid (Ezra 3:10-13) and while the temple was under construction (Hag. 2:3).

God gave a clear promise that Zerubbabel would complete the temple (Zech.4:9), which reminds us of God's promise in Philippians 1:6, "Being confident of this very thing, that He who has begun a good work in you will complete it until the day of Jesus Christ" (NKJV). It also echoes David's words to his son Solomon: "Be strong and of good courage, and do it; do not fear nor be dismayed, for the Lord God—my God— will be with you. He will not leave you nor forsake you, until you have finished all the work for the service of the house of the Lord" (1 Chron. 28:20, NKJV). That was the promise that sustained me during my first building program in my first pastorate, and I can assure you that—it works!

To some of the Jews, the project was but a "small thing" (Zech. 4:10) in comparison to Solomon's grand temple, but we must look at God's work through His eyes and not the eyes of the people of the world. Great oaks grow out of small acorns and great harvests from small seeds. When Messiah came to earth, He was but "a shoot...from the stump of Jesse" (Isa. 11:1, NIV) and was "despised and rejected of men" (Isa. 53:3). The church began with 120 people and today ministers around the world.

Bible history is the record of God using small things. When God wanted to set the plan of salvation in motion, He started with a little baby named Isaac (Gen. 21). When He wanted to overthrow Egypt and set His people free, He used a baby's tears (Ex. 2:1-10). He used a shepherd boy and a sling to defeat a giant (1 Sam. 17) and a little lad's lunch to feed a multitude (John 6). He delivered the Apostle Paul from death by using a basket and a rope (Acts 9:23-25). Never despise the day of small things, for God is glorified in small things and uses them to accomplish great things.

God and His servants must work together to accomplish His purposes. "For it is God who works in you both to will and to do for His good pleasure" (Phil. 2:13, NKJV). God supplies His servants with the Spirit, and the people are encouraged as they see Zerubbabel on the job with the plumb line in his hand, making sure the walls are straight. While

Zerubbabel is working, the eyes of the Lord are watching over His people and monitoring the nations of the earth. (The phrase "those seven" in Zech. 4:10 refers back to 3:9, the eyes of the Lord, meaning His omniscience.)

The vision climaxes (4:14) with God calling Zerubbabel and Joshua "the two anointed ones, that stand by the Lord of the whole earth." What a noble title for His servants! As the two olive trees, Joshua and Zerubbabel received the empowering Spirit of God and kept the light of Israel's work and witness burning. Oil is a general symbol for the Holy Spirit in Scripture. Prophets, priests, and kings were anointed with oil, and the words "Messiah" and "Christ" mean "anointed one." The holy anointing oil was not to be prepared by anybody but the priests or be used for any other purpose than for anointing God's servants (Ex. 30:22-33). "The Spirit of the Lord God is upon Me, because the Lord has anointed Me" (Isa. 61:1; Luke 4:18-19).

If our God is "Lord of all the earth," what have we to fear? If He promises us the power of His Spirit, why should we falter and fail? Let's remember Joshua and Zerubbabel, men who are encouragements to all who seek to serve the Lord in any way.

There are no "small places" or "small ministries," and there are no "big preachers." But we do have a great God who can empower and bless servants who are dedicated to Him. He can cleanse us and He can empower us, so let's trust Him and do His work!

God and the Nations

The previous vision ended with the interpreting angel calling Israel's God "the Lord of the whole earth" (4:14), a title that is also used in Psalm 95:7 and Isaiah 54:5. Zechariah's purpose in writing is to tell us about the future of the Jews and Jerusalem, but the future of *the whole world* is involved in the future of the Jews, for God called Israel to bring blessing or cursing to all the nations of the earth (Gen. 12:1-3).

The prophet describes three key events that give evidence that the God of Abraham, Isaac, and Jacob is indeed "the Lord of the whole earth."

1. The cleansing of the land (Zech. 5:1-11)

The vision of the flying scroll and the vision of the ephah focus primarily on the land of Israel.[1] In both of them, God performs a cleansing operation and deals with the sins of the nation.

God removes lawlessness (vv. 1-4). The prophet saw a large open scroll, fifteen feet by thirty feet, floating through the air, with writing on both sides. On one side he read the third commandment against taking God's name in vain (Ex. 20:7), and on the other side he read the eighth commandment against stealing (v. 15).

This scroll represented the Law of God that brings a curse on all who disobey it, and that includes all of us (Deut. 27:26; Gal. 3:10-12); because nobody can fully obey God's law. For that matter, the law was never given to save people (Gal. 2:16, 21; 3:21) but to reveal that people need to be saved; "for by the law is the knowledge of sin" (Rom. 3:20).

Out of Ten Commandments, why did the Lord select the two that forbid stealing and swearing falsely? Were these sins especially prevalent among the Jewish remnant at that time? It may be that many of the Jewish people were not faithful in their giving to the Lord, robbing Him of tithes and offerings and then lying about it. In their business dealings, they may have cheated one another. The Prophet Haggai rebuked them for putting their own interests ahead of the Lord's work (Hag. 1:1-11), and certainly robbing God was a grievous sin among the Jews a century later (Mal. 3:7-15).

But there is another reason. The third commandment is the central commandment on the first table of the Law, and the eighth commandment is the central commandment on the second table of the law, so these two commandments represent the whole law. "But whoever shall keep the whole law, yet offend in one point, he is guilty of all" (James 2:10).

If I'm suspended over a chasm by a chain of ten links, how many links have to break before I fall? If while driving down the highway, I'm pulled over by a policeman because I'm speeding, does it make any difference to him that I haven't broken the income tax laws or stolen anything from my neighbors? Obedience to one law doesn't negate disobedience to another law. To break one is to become a lawless person.

God announced that the scroll of His law would visit the individual homes in the land and judge those who were deliberately disobeying God. Whether "cut off" means killed or expelled from the covenant community isn't made clear. Like a thief or a plague, the curse would enter the houses unannounced and bring destruction.

The Jewish remnant was certainly familiar with the "blessings and curses" of the covenant recorded by Moses. They also knew that after Joshua had brought the people into the Promised Land, they gathered at Mount Ebal and Mount Gerizim and read the "blessings and curses" and promised to obey the Lord (Josh. 8:30-35).

Lawlessness abounds today and the only commandment many people worry about is "Thou shalt not get caught!" Ethics is something studied in the classroom but not seriously practiced in the marketplace, and the Ten Commandments are only dusty artifacts in the museum of morality. No wonder Hosea wrote, "They make many promises, take false oaths and make agreements; therefore lawsuits spring up like poisonous weeds in a plowed field" (10:4, NIV). People break God's law and then try to use man's law to protect themselves, and often they win!

Ultimately, God will judge *all* sinners who have rebelled against His law (Jude 14-15); but He will start with Israel, the nation that gave us God's Law. It's a divine principle that judgment begins with God's people (1 Peter 4:17; Ezek. 9:6). This judgment will occur before our Lord establishes His kingdom on earth, and the "holy land" will truly become holy (Zech. 2:12). God will "remove the iniquity of the land in one day" (Zech. 3:9).

God removes wickedness (5:6-11). Not only will individual sins and sinners be judged, but wickedness itself will be removed from the land. In this vision, wickedness is personified by a woman, because the Hebrew word for "wickedness" is feminine. The ephah was a common measure in Israel, but no ephah would be large enough to house a person, so, like the huge scroll, this was a special ephah. The woman attempted to get out of the ephah, so a heavy lead cover was put on the ephah to keep her in. A talent of lead would weigh from seventy-five to one hundred pounds.

The prophet then saw two other women, but they had wings! With the help of the wind, they lifted up the basket and its contents, plus the heavy lead cover, and carried it in the air to Babylon. Although angels are actually sexless (Matt. 22:30), in Scripture they are generally depicted as male, so these two women were special agents of the Lord created just for this particular task. They took the ephah and the woman to Shinar (Babylon, Dan. 1:2) and put the ephah on a base in a special house.

In order to understand this vision, we must ask ourselves, "What did the Jews bring to their land from Babylon when they returned after their captivity?" It wasn't idolatry, for their years of exile cured them of that sin. The answer is—*commercialism*. The Jews were people of the land when they went to Babylon, but many of the Jews born in Babylon became people of the city and successful merchants. So it was the spirit of competitive commercialism that was represented by the woman in the ephah, for both the ephah and the talent are measures of commodities.

The ancient city of Babylon is first mentioned in Genesis 10:10 as a part of Nimrod's empire. Nimrod is called "a mighty one in the earth" and "a mighty hunter" (Gen. 10:8-9), which the NIV translates "a mighty warrior...a mighty hunter." This is the picture of a conquering despot, forging himself a kingdom at any cost and defying the Lord in the process. The famous Tower of Babel was built in Shinar as an attempt to exalt man and dethrone God (11:1-19).

Throughout Scripture, Babylon symbolizes the world's enmity against God, culminating in the vivid description in Revelation 17–18. (See also the parallel in Jer. 50–51.) The contrast in the Book of Revelation is between the Bride (the heavenly city) and the harlot (the earthly city of Babylon). When you read Revelation 18, you see that the emphasis is on the commercial success and the vast wealth of Babylon, the very "virus" that some of the Jews had caught during the Babylonian exile.

This doesn't imply that the people of Israel today are all guilty of bad business practices, or that it's wrong for anybody to earn money by engaging in business. Both believers and unbelievers, Jews or Gentiles, can be manufacturers and merchants and faithfully do their work. But if the worldly commercial spirit infects the child of God, it will result in twisted values, confused priorities, and a craving for wealth and position that grieves the Lord (1 Tim. 6). The best antidote is Matthew 6:33.

The two women with storklike wings placed the ephah on a base in a special house in Babylon, which suggests that "commercialism" was worshiped as one of the Babylonian gods. Unfortunately, money has become a god around the world and, like a god, money is trusted by people to give them help, to solve their problems, to provide happiness, and to empower them to accomplish their goals in life. The last of the Ten Commandments is "Thou shalt not covet" (Ex. 20:17), but coveting will cause people to break the other nine commandments. "For the love of money is a root of all kinds of evil" (1 Tim. 6:10, NKJV), everything from lying on one's income tax to murdering a helpless victim for a few dollars.

God has now cleansed the land. What is His next step in preparing His people for their promised kingdom?

2. God judges the nations (Zech. 6:1-8)

The images in this vision are similar to those described in 1:7-17, but the details are significantly different. The emphasis here is on the horses and chariots rather than the riders, and their ministry is that of accomplishing God's purposes rather than reporting on conditions in the Gentile world. In the first vision, there were many horses and riders but here, there are only four chariots, each with their horses.

The four chariots with their horses represented the "four spirits" from God, that is, four angels (Heb. 1:14) assigned to different parts of the world to do God's bidding. "The chariots of God are twenty thousand, even thousands of angels" (Ps. 68:17). The presence of chariots suggests battle, and this implies judgment. "For behold, the Lord will come with fire and with His chariots, like a whirlwind, to render [bring down, NIV] His anger with fury, and His rebuke with flames of fire" (Isa. 66:15, NKJV).

If the horses' colors are significant, then Revelation 6:1-8 can assist us. The red horses symbolize war; the black horses, famine; and the white horses, death. There are no dappled horses in the vision John had in Revelation 6, but they could well symbolize plagues. During the "Day of the Lord," God will use wars, famines, plagues, and death to punish the nations of the earth.

Since the two mountains (Zech. 6:1) were made of bronze, they are symbolic, for there are no bronze mountains in the Holy Land or anywhere else. In Scripture, bronze often symbolizes judgment. The altar of sacrifice in the tabernacle and the temple was made of wood covered with bronze, and that's where sin was judged when the sacrifices were burned. The serpent that Moses put on the pole was made of bronze (Num. 21:9), and when our Lord appeared to John and was about to judge the churches, His feet were compared to bronze "as if they burned in a furnace" (Rev. 1:15).

So, the cumulative effect of this vision is that God will judge the Gentile nations for their sins. This will occur during the period of time called "the Tribulation" or "the Day of the Lord" which precedes the return of Christ to the earth to set up His righteous kingdom. In the latter chapters of his book, Zechariah will describe many of the events that will occur during "the day of the Lord."

When Zechariah saw the horses, they were straining to go to their appointed destinations and do what God had ordered them to do. However, judgment is in the hands of God, reserved for the right time and place (see Rev. 9:15). The black horses were assigned to the north country (Babylon) and the white horses would follow them, while the dappled horses would go to the south (Egypt). Nothing is said about the red horses, so apparently the Lord was holding them back for another time. [2] God was angry with the nations in the north (Zech. 6:8; see 1:15), and His messengers would see to it that His holy purposes there were fulfilled. This would bring peace to God's heart as His justice was satisfied.

The ministry of angels among the nations and in dispensing God's judgments is clearly taught in other parts of Scripture (Dan. 4:4-18; 10; 12:1; Rev. 8; 14; 16). Zechariah's vision assures us that God is in control of the future and will judge the Gentile nations during "the Day of the Lord." God is long-suffering (2 Peter 3:9), but there comes a time when nations "fill up the measure of their sins" (Gen. 15:16; Matt. 23:32); and then God's judgment must fall.

3. God crowns His King-Priest (Zech. 6:9-15)

The eight visions came to an end, but there was yet another message from God to His servant. In the visions, God had assured His people that He would cleanse them and protect them from their enemies. But there was a message for the future as well. During the "Day of the Lord," the nations would be punished for their sins, but Israel would be delivered. At the climax of that day, Messiah would return, the Jews would see Him and trust Him, and the nation would be cleansed. Then Messiah would be crowned as King-Priest to reign over His righteous kingdom (Zech. 9–14).

Confrontation (6:9-11). We aren't told when God gave Zechariah these instructions, but it was probably shortly after he had seen the eight visions, for this event is really the climax of the revelations given in the visions.

God told Zechariah that three esteemed Jews would arrive from Babylon, bringing gold and silver offerings to the Lord for the building of the temple. They would stay at the home of Josiah, who had the wonderful nickname "Hen," which means "gracious one" (v. 14). After they arrived in Jerusalem, Zechariah went to see them.

We can only imagine what transpired when the prophet told the visitors what God had commanded him to do: take their silver and gold offerings and make an elaborate crown.[3] He was then to put this crown, not on the head of Zerubbabel the governor, who was of the royal line of David, but on the head of Joshua the high priest!

The visitors no doubt faced two problems: (1) the money from the Jews in Babylon was supposed to be used for the completion of the temple; and (2) there was no precedent in Scripture for a priest to be crowned king. Was Zechariah trying to oust the governor and make Joshua ruler of the struggling nation? How would this better the situation of the remnant and hasten the completion of the temple?

Coronation (vv. 12-13). Zechariah saved the explanation until he had fully obeyed the Lord. He made the crown and, taking the visitors with him, went to Joshua the high priest and conducted a coronation service. We don't know if all the elders of Israel were invited, but since the message this act conveyed was such an important one, it's likely that they were.

Then Zechariah explained God's message to the high priest and the witnesses. He must have told them that both Zerubbabel and Joshua were "men symbolic of things to come" (Zech. 3:8, NIV). Even though Zerubbabel was from David's line, he wasn't the one God chose to be crowned. God chose Joshua and for the first time in Jewish history, the Lord united the monarchy and the priesthood.

All of this refers, of course, to Jesus Christ; for He is "the man whose name is the Branch" (6:12; see 3:8).[4] Looking down to the time of the kingdom, God announced that Messiah would be both King and Priest: He would sit on the throne and reign, but He would also build the temple and serve as a priest. In fact, many Jews and Gentiles will come from afar off and help build the millennial temple (6:15; Isa. 60:5-12; Hag. 2:7-9).

No priest in Jewish history ever served as king; and the one king, Uzziah, who tried to become a priest, was severely judged by the Lord (2 Chron. 26:16-21). Only in Messiah does Jehovah unite both the throne and the altar. Today, Jesus Christ serves in heaven as both King and Priest, ministering "after the order of Melchizedek" (Heb. 7–8). This is in fulfillment of the Father's promise to the Son recorded in Psalm 110:4.

But during the reign of Christ on earth, there will be a restored temple and priesthood (Isa. 2:1-5; 27:13; Ezek. 40–48; Zech. 14:16), and Jesus Christ will sit on the throne of His father David as King and Priest (Luke 1:32-33).[5] This will be the fulfillment of God's covenant promise to David that he would always have an heir seated on his throne (2 Sam. 7).

The statement in Zechariah 6:13 that "the counsel of peace shall be between them both" is translated in the NIV, "And there will be harmony between the two." In the kingdom, there will be perfect peace and justice because all civil and religious authority will be harmonized in one Person, Messiah, the King and Priest.

Commemoration (vv.14-15). Zechariah then took the crown from off Joshua's head and gave him his priestly miter (3:5). Why? Because the symbolic act was over and the crown did not belong to Joshua. It belonged to the coming Messiah. Zechariah placed the crown somewhere in the temple as a memorial (reminder) of the Lord's promise of a King-Priest who would bring peace and holiness to His people.

God will be faithful to His promises even if His people are unfaithful (2 Tim. 2:12-13), but they will miss out on the blessings. He didn't put any conditions on the wonderful promise of a future King-Priest, but Zechariah 6:15 seems to limit God's working to the obedience of His people. "This will happen if you diligently obey the Lord your God" (NIV).

This statement is a reference to God's covenant recorded in Deuteronomy 28: "Now it shall come to pass, if you diligently obey the voice of the Lord your God" (v. 1). The remnant of Jews then in the Holy Land had to obey God's laws so that He might protect them and bless them as He promised, for the Messiah had to be born from this nation. Within a few centuries, the Angel Gabriel would visit Mary and tell her she had been chosen to bring the promised Messiah into the world (Luke 1:26-38). The faithfulness of one generation assured the blessing of the next generations and ultimately the blessing of the whole world.

The visions are ended. We have seen a vivid panorama of God's plans for Israel, culminating in the King-Priest on David's throne, ruling over Israel and the whole world.

Remember these prophecies the next time you pray, "Thy kingdom come."

Truth, Traditions, and Promises

To what extent do the traditions of the past have authority over what the church does today? As times change, should customs also change? And who has the authority to change them? Are religious traditions to remain as they've always been, or can we drop the old ones and begin some new ones?

These are questions that are challenging churches today and even dividing churches, but these questions aren't new. Similar questions were asked centuries ago when Sharezer and Regemelech arrived in Jerusalem from Babylon. The Jews in Babylon had sent them to ask the Prophet Zechariah about the traditional Jewish fasts. Zechariah used the opportunity to teach the people about true spiritual worship, and then he turned their eyes away from the past to the promises of the future.

1. Problems concerning tradition (Zech. 7:1-14)

Tradition is a useful and necessary social practice. It helps to tie generations together and keep society moving in a united way. Whether the traditions involve the way we eat and dress, how we treat our parents and family, the way we move from childhood into maturity, or the way we choose a job or a mate, tradition helps to stabilize things and guide us in making acceptable choices. But sometimes tradition creates problems, especially when the times change radically and people don't want to change with the times.

The request (vv. 1-3). Almost two years had elapsed since the crowning of Joshua and the work of rebuilding the temple had gone on steadily. In another three years, the temple would be completed and dedicated. While we have no recorded messages from Zechariah during that time, certainly he was ministering to the people and encouraging the workers in their important task.

The Law of Moses required the Jews to observe only one national fast, and that was on the annual Day of Atonement (Lev. 23:16-32). Of course, individual Jews could fast from time to time as they felt led, but this wasn't required of the entire nation.

To commemorate events surrounding the destruction of Jerusalem and the temple, four new fasts had been added to the religious calendar by the Jewish exiles in Babylon (see Zech. 8:19): one in the tenth month, when the Babylonians had begun the siege of the city; another in the fourth month, when the city walls had been broken through; one in the fifth month, when the temple was burned; and the fourth in the seventh month, when the Jewish governor Gedaliah had been assassinated (see Jer. 41).

The significant question was: "Now that the temple was being rebuilt, was it necessary to continue the fast in the fifth month that commemorated the burning of the temple?"

The reply (Zech. 7:4-7). Zechariah didn't give them an immediate reply. In fact, the Lord didn't reveal His will in the matter until later (8:9). It was necessary first to deal with the heart attitudes of the people. After all, our relationship with the Lord isn't so much a matter of traditions and rules as it is faith, love, and a desire to please Him. Immature people require religious regulations to tell them what to do, and these regulations help them measure their "spiritual life." But God wants us to mature spiritually and grow from obeying rules to following principles and cultivating a vital personal relationship with Him.

In true rabbinical fashion, Zechariah answered their question by *asking* some questions! In fact, he asked these questions of all the people and priests, for they too had kept these fasts. "When you fasted," Zechariah asked, "did you do it for the Lord or for yourselves? And when you feasted, was it for the Lord or for yourselves? What was in your heart?"

The prophets who ministered prior to the fall of Jerusalem had taught the people that their religious observances had to come from the heart. To worship God any other way meant to practice hypocrisy. As far back as the ministry of Samuel, God told the people that He wanted their obedience and not their sacrifices (1 Sam. 15:22), and this truth was also taught in the Psalms (50:8-14; 51:16). Isaiah had proclaimed this message (Isa. 1:11-17; 58:1-14), and so did the Prophet Micah (6:6-8), but the people didn't listen. Life was peaceful and secure in those days, and it was much easier to maintain the traditions than to really meet with God and have a "heart experience" of worship.

Zechariah wasn't condemning traditions as such. He was emphasizing the fact that the true spiritual life can't be turned on and off at our convenience, so that we serve God one minute and forget Him the next. If we feast, we must do it to glorify God (1 Cor. 10:31); if we fast, we must do it to honor Him. The Lord must be the center of our lives and the reason for our actions. If we keep a fast (or any other religious tradition) just to please ourselves and win the admiration and approval of others, then God was not pleased and the activity was wasted.

God's final answer was given later (Zech. 8:19): all four fasts will one day be turned into feasts! This would take place during the Kingdom Age when Messiah will sit on the throne, judging with justice and truth. (Isaiah saw the same picture; Isa. 61:2-3; 65:19.) So, instead of living in the past tense and mourning over calamities, why not live in the future tense and rejoice over what God has promised to do for His people?

The rebuke (Zech. 7:8-14). Zechariah reminded the people of the way their forefathers routinely practiced their religion but failed to hear God's Word and obey it from their hearts. That was the reason Jerusalem and the temple had been destroyed. Their "religion" was just a part of their lives; it wasn't the very heart of their lives. They could go to the temple and piously present their prayers and sacrifices, but then leave the temple to break God's Law, worship idols, and abuse other people.

Through the prophets, the Lord had called the people to practice justice, but the leaders had continued to exploit the people for personal gain. The rulers of the nation had ignored the Law of Moses and refused to show compassion toward the poor, the widows and orphans, and the aliens in the land (Ex. 22:22-24; Deut. 10:18-22; Amos 2:6-8; 5:11-12, 21-24). God wasn't interested in their sacrifices and prayers so much as the obedience of their hearts.

The danger of tradition is that it can easily turn into *traditionalism*. "Tradition is the living faith of the dead," wrote theologian Jerislav Pelikan; "traditionalism is the dead faith of the living." Traditionalism means going through the outward motions instead of honoring the Lord from our heart; it means participating in a religious event but failing to have an inner spiritual experience.

Sometimes the only way the Lord can bring us back to reality is to force us to endure suffering. "Before I was afflicted I went astray, but now I have kept Thy word" (Ps. 119:67). When we find ourselves in the furnace of affliction, we turn to God and His promises, because that's the only hope we have. The Lord had to send the Jewish people into exile before they'd learn to turn from idols and appreciate all the blessings they had because of God's grace.

The word "tradition" simply means "that which is passed along." It comes from a Latin word that means "to hand over." The basic doctrines of the Christian faith must be handed from generation to generation (1 Tim. 2:2; 1 John 1:1-3; 1 Cor. 11:2; 1 Thes. 2:15; 3:6; Jude 3), but the customs and traditions of the early church don't carry the same authority as the inspired Word of God. In fact, as times change, some of these customs may be detrimental to the work of the Lord. To institute four fasts because of the tragedies that occurred in Jerusalem, *and yet not repent because of the sins that caused these tragedies,* was to miss the whole purpose of God's discipline.

Centuries ago, when the first missionaries went to Moravia, they weren't allowed to preach in the Slavic language! Why? Because the only "holy languages" the church approved were Hebrew, Greek, and Latin. Fortunately, the church leaders had sense enough to revoke this foolish edict; otherwise, evangelism would have been impossible. Believers today who insist that we sing only the Psalms in our public worship, accompanied only by an organ or a piano, are captive to traditions that have no biblical basis. City congregations that follow a Sunday time schedule that was tailored for the rural community may be losing opportunities to reach urbanites with the Gospel. Over the years, I've been privileged to minister in many churches of different denominations, and I've seen how dead traditions can become roadblocks to progress.

Churches are like families; each one has its own set of traditions, many of which may be good. The truths of God's Word don't change, but changing circumstances reveal new principles and new applications of that Word. The old Youth for Christ slogan said it perfectly: we must be "geared to the times, but anchored to the Rock."

Jesus dealt with the question of tradition when He was ministering here on earth (Matt. 15; Mark 7). He carefully distinguished between the inspired Word of God that never changes and man-made traditions that are always subject to review and revision. Final authority for faith and practice must rest in the Word of God. "Tradition is a guide and not a jailer," wrote novelist W. Somerset Maugham, but history reveals that it's a difficult thing for many people to break with tradition. It's easier to have a religion of habit than a religion of the heart. Churches, families, and individual believers need to examine their cherished traditions in the light of God's truth. Perhaps some of our fasts need to be turned into feasts! (Zech. 8:18)

2. Promises concerning Israel (Zech. 8:1-23)

God's people don't live on explanations; they live on promises. Faith and hope are nourished by the promises of God given to us in the Scriptures. That explains why Zechariah dropped the discussion of the traditions and delivered a new message from the Lord. In this message, he focused the people's eyes of faith on the future and shared some wonderful promises to encourage them. Note the repetition of the phrase, "Thus saith the Lord," which is used ten times in this chapter.

The city of Jerusalem will be rebuilt (vv. 1-6). God affirmed His jealous love and concern for Zion, just as He had done earlier (1:14). He promises that Jerusalem will be rebuilt and become a wholly different city, dedicated to truth and holiness. This promise will be fulfilled when Jesus Christ returns to earth to establish His kingdom (Isa. 1:26; 2:3;

60:14; 62:12).

But the compassionate Lord centers on *people* and not *buildings,* particularly the elderly and the children. He describes a city so safe and friendly that the elderly can leisurely sit in the streets and talk, and where the children can play in the streets and not be in danger. In today's man-made cities, the elderly and the children aren't safe in the streets or anywhere else! The children are killed before they have a chance to be born, and when the elderly are no longer "useful," we find legal ways to end their lives. But all of that will change when Jesus returns and righteousness reigns.[1]

The people of Israel will be regathered (Zech. 7:7). True to His covenant, God disciplined His disobedient people and dispersed them throughout the world (Deut. 28:63); but one day, He will regather them to their land and to their holy city (Isa. 11:11-12; 43:5-7; Jer. 30:7-11; 31:7-8). While groups of Jewish patriots have returned from time to time to their land, the kind of worldwide regathering described by the prophets has never yet occurred.

The relationship between Israel and Jehovah will be restored (Zech. 7:8). The promise "They will be My people" reminds us that God claimed the people of Israel as His own. When God delivered Israel from Egyptian bondage, He said to them, "Obey My voice, and do according to all that I command you; so shall you be My people, and I will be your God" (Jer. 11:4, NKJV; see Ex. 19:3-5). For a time, God abandoned His people because they abandoned Him, and He called them "Lo-ammi; for you are not My people, and I will not be your God" (Hosea 1:9, NKJV).

The nation of Israel was punished for her idolatry by being sent into Babylonian captivity. Then she was punished for rejecting her Messiah by being sent into worldwide dispersion. One day, God will summon His sons and daughters from afar and the streets of a restored Jerusalem will be crowded with His people. "At that time I will gather you; at that time I will bring you home. I will give you honor and praise among all the peoples of the earth when I restore your fortunes before your very eyes" (Zeph. 3:20).

The land of Israel will be refreshed (7:9-13). Haggai had rebuked the Jewish remnant because the people weren't faithful to the Lord in their stewardship (Hag. 1). Instead of honoring the Lord and building His house, they built their own houses first, and for this sin, God disciplined them. The weather turned bad, their crops failed, and the economy became worse and worse. God wasn't being unkind to His people; He was only being true to His covenant (Deut. 28:38-46).

But now the land would be refreshed by the Lord and the crops would grow abundantly. Laborers would get their wages and their money would be sufficient to pay their bills. The Lord would send the promised rain (Deut. 28:11-12) and the other nations would witness the blessing of the Lord on His people. Instead of being a reproach, Israel would become a witness to the glory of the Lord.

While this promise of material blessing was given primarily to the remnant in Zechariah's day, it has its application to the future regathered and restored nation. God promises that "the desert shall rejoice and blossom like the rose" (Isa. 35:1) in the kingdom of Messiah.

There are two facts about material blessings that we must always keep in mind. First, we don't obey God just to become wealthy and secure. We obey God because He is God and deserves our loving obedience. Obedience builds character, and when our character is what it ought to be, God can trust us with His blessings. Material blessings aren't bribes, nor are they rewards. They're God's way of saying, "You're maturing in godliness, and now I can give you more to use for My glory."

Second, God doesn't always respond with material blessings, and poverty is not a sign that God has forsaken His people. The experience of Job completely destroys this "commercial" idea of faith and obedience. Job's friends had a "commercial" view of faith, so they encouraged Job to confess his sins so God could again make him wealthy. Bargain with God! But Job refused to do that, though he didn't understand what the Lord was working out in his sufferings.

God's covenant with Israel declared that He would punish them physically and materially if they disobeyed Him, but bless them if they obeyed Him (Deut. 27–28; Lev. 26). However, He has no such covenant with Christian believers today. He promises to meet all our needs (Phil. 4:19) and direct in all our circumstances (Rom. 8:28), but our riches are of a heavenly nature (Eph. 1:3). If God chooses to make some of His people wealthy, it's that they might use what He gives them to help others (1 Tim. 6:17-19). He blesses us that we might be a blessing. However, riches are no proof of God's special love, nor is poverty evidence that He's forsaken us.

The covenant standards will be renewed (vv. 14-19). Whether God is dealing with His people in the Old Testament or the New Testament, His standards don't change. The church today doesn't live under Old Covenant law, but "the righteousness of the law" is still what God wants to develop in our lives (Rom. 8:1-4). "Be holy, for I am holy" is quoted from the Old Testament law for New Testament Christians (Lev. 11:44; 1 Peter 1:15-16).

God reminded His people of their obligations to speak the truth, to practice justice in the courts, to honor His name by not swearing falsely, and to love their neighbors. Of course, all the law is fulfilled in our conduct when we practice love (Rom. 13:8-10). The God of love hates sin! (See Prov.

6:16-19.) God's dispensations may change, and He can work in different ways at different times, but His character and standards never change. He wants His people to be "a holy nation" (Ex. 19:6; 1 Peter 2:9). "Therefore, love the truth and peace" (Zech. 7:19).

In verse 18, the prophet clearly answered the question about the fasts. The day would come when Messiah would reign and all Israel's fasts would become feasts! "And I will rejoice in Jerusalem, and joy in my people; and the voice of weeping shall be no more heard in her, nor the voice of crying" (Isa. 65:19). Zechariah and Isaiah were both saying, "Don't live in the past tense; live in the future tense! Rejoice at the promises God gives you for a joyful future!"[2]

The Gentiles will be redeemed (Zech. 7:20-23). God called Abraham and established the nation of Israel so His people would witness to the Gentiles and lead them to faith in the true God (Gen. 12:1-3). In setting apart one nation, God was seeking to reach a whole world. Many of the great events in Jewish history recorded in Scripture had behind them a witness to "the whole world": the plagues of Egypt (Ex. 9:16); the conquest of Canaan (Josh. 4:23-24); God's blessing of the nation (Deut. 28:9-11); and even the building of the temple (1 Kings 8:42-43). When David killed Goliath, he announced that God would give him victory so "that all the earth may know that there is a God in Israel" (1 Sam. 17:46).

But Israel failed in her mission to the Gentiles. Instead of the Gentile nations coming to worship the true God of Israel, the Jews forsook Jehovah and worshiped the false gods of the Gentile nations. The "court of the Gentiles" in Herod's temple became a market where Jews visiting Jerusalem from other countries could exchange their money and buy approved sacrifices. However, before we criticize the Jews too much, we had better examine the track record of the church when it comes to winning the lost at home and taking the Gospel to nations abroad.

When Messiah restores His people and establishes His kingdom, the Gentiles will trust the true and living God and come to Jerusalem to worship Him. Isaiah saw a river of Gentiles "flowing" into the city (Isa. 2:1-5) and Micah used the same figure (Micah 4:1-5). Zechariah describes a scene in which ten men (a Hebrew expression for "many men") will take hold of one Jew and beg to go with him to the temple!

It's a wonderful thing when God so blesses His people that others want what God's people have. "We have heard that God is with you" (Zech. 7:23). This sounds like what should happen in our local churches when an unbeliever beholds our worship of the Lord. "He will be convinced by all that he is a sinner and will be judged by all, and the secrets of his heart will be laid bare. So he will fall down and worship God, exclaiming, 'God is really among you!" (1 Cor. 14:24-25, NIV)

"I say then," wrote Paul, "has God cast away His people? Certainly not!" (Rom. 11:1, NKJV) There's a bright and blessed future for God's people Israel, even though the nation has been oppressed and persecuted by the Gentiles, some of whom claimed to be Christians. Our privilege is to love them, pray for them, and tell them that their Messiah, Jesus Christ, has come and will save them if they trust in Him.[3] The Gospel of Christ is still "the power of God for salvation to everyone who believes, for the Jew first and also for the Greek" (Rom. 1:16, NKJV).

Messiah, the Shepherd-King

In the last half of his book, Zechariah presents two oracles ("burdens")[1] that focus on the first and second advents of the coming Messiah. These six chapters comprise one of the greatest concentrations of messianic truth found anywhere in Scripture, but the truth is always related to God's purposes for His people Israel. Zechariah reveals Messiah as the humble King, the loving Shepherd, the mighty Warrior, the gracious Savior, and the righteous Ruler who will reign on earth as King and Priest.

Bible students may not agree on the interpretation of each detail of these complex prophecies, but they do agree on the greatness of the Christ whose character and ministry are so vividly portrayed here. As we study these chapters, may our hearts burn within us (Luke 24:32) and may we love Him more.

1. Messiah's first advent (Zech. 9:1-9)

The coming of God's Son to this earth wasn't heaven's "Plan B" or a hasty decision by the Father after our first parents sinned. The plan of redemption was settled in eternity, before there ever was a creation. The coming of the Lamb of

God was "foreordained before the foundation of the world" (1 Peter 1:20), for He was "the Lamb slain from the foundation of the world" (Rev. 13:8).

Preparation for the King (Zech. 9:1-8). These verses describe the march of Alexander the Great and his army through the area north and east of Palestine. Alexander defeated the Persians in 333 B.C. at the Battle of Issus and then turned to conquer the leading cities in Phoenicia. Daniel had predicted Alexander's success; he compared him to a winged leopard (Dan. 7:6) and a fighting he-goat (Dan. 8). It's been said that prophecy is history pre-written, and both Daniel and Zechariah wrote some of that history.

Hadrach was a region to the far north of Palestine, bordered by the Euphrates River, and Damascus was the capital of Syria. After defeating these nations, the Greek army then marched down the Phoenician coast, taking one city after another, from Tyre and Sidon in the north to Ashkelon and Gaza in the south. Indeed, God "cut off the pride of the Philistines" (Zech. 9:6) and put an end to their idolatrous worship (v. 7). [2]

The statement in verse 1 about "the eyes of men being toward the Lord" may mean that Alexander's victorious march caused people to look to God for help, but it could also mean that God's eyes were on the nations and especially on His people Israel. The NIV marginal translation says, "For the eye of the Lord is on all mankind, as well as on the tribes of Israel." Merrill Unger suggests that as the people were watching Alexander, they were actually watching God at work, for "history is His story."

After a two-month siege of Gaza, Alexander took the city and then went to Jerusalem. [3] He was unhappy with the Jews because they had refused to pay him the annual tribute that they usually gave to the Persians. The high priest in Jerusalem called for the people to fast and pray, and he presented sacrifices to the Lord to seek His special protection.

The night before Alexander and his army were to arrive at Jerusalem, the high priest had a dream in which God told him to adorn the city, tell the people to dress in white garments, and open the gates to their visitor. The high priest and the other priests would head the procession dressed in their holy robes. This they did, and Alexander was so impressed that he welcomed them in peace. The high priest told Alexander about Daniel's prophecies concerning him, and Alexander even offered sacrifices to Jehovah in the temple. Thus, the city and the people were spared.

But Zechariah had promised that Jerusalem and Judea would be spared. "I will camp around My house because of the army, because of him who passes by and him who returns" (v. 8, NKJV). Alexander had passed by Jerusalem en route to Gaza, but then he turned back to the Holy City. How much of Josephus' account is fact and how much is tradition, we can't tell, but we do know that God kept His promise and protected His people.

But why all this concern over the conquests of Alexander the Great? *His conquests helped to prepare the world for the coming of Jesus Christ.* By building Greek cities, encouraging his soldiers to marry women from conquered nations, and spreading Greek culture and the Greek language, he unified the known world, and when the Romans took over, they found an empire all prepared for them. Greek was the language of literature, and our New Testament is written in the common Greek language of the people of that day. The combination of Greek culture and Roman government, roads, and laws was just what the early church needed for the spread of the Gospel.

However, the promise in verse 8 goes far beyond the time of Alexander, for it states that God is always protecting His people and His house. No one can touch them without His permission. In the centuries since Alexander's conquest, the Jewish nation has suffered often because of invaders, and Jerusalem and the temple were destroyed by the Romans in A.D. 70. But the day will come when Messiah will reign and no invader will be able to threaten God's people let alone attack them.

Presentation of the King (v. 9). This prophecy was fulfilled when Jesus Christ rode into Jerusalem on what we traditionally call "Palm Sunday," and the event is recorded in all four Gospels (Matt. 21:1-11; Mark 11:1-11; Luke 19:29-44; and John 12:12-19). This is the only public demonstration Jesus allowed during His ministry, and He did it to fulfill Scripture.

When Zechariah put this prophecy about Jesus right after his prophecy concerning Alexander the Great, he was obviously inviting his readers to contrast the two conquerors. Alexander's arrival brought fear to people, but the Jews were commanded to rejoice and shout because their King had come. Jesus was righteous in all that He did, and His purpose in coming was to bring salvation to those who would trust Him. How different from Alexander!

Alexander rode a mighty steed and proudly led a great army from one victory to another, but Jesus rode a lowly donkey and came in humility. [4] The people who welcomed Him were common peasants who laid palm branches and garments before Him on the road. The great people of Jerusalem didn't welcome Him, but little children sang to Him in the temple. Jesus could have brought judgment, but instead He brought grace and forgiveness (John 3:17). Instead of making a grand oration, Jesus beheld the city and wept over it; instead of slaying His enemies, *He went to a cross and died for them!*

What a wonderful Conqueror! Let's move now to the future and examine His conquests.

2. Messiah's conquests at His second advent (Zech. 9:10–10:12)

The entire age of the church fits between Zechariah 9:9 and 9:10, just as it does between Isaiah 9:6 and 7 and after the comma in Isaiah 61:2. The prophet is now writing about what will happen when Jesus comes to earth to defeat His enemies and establish His kingdom. At His first advent, He rode a humble donkey; but at His second advent, He will ride a white horse and lead the armies of heaven (Rev. 19:11-21).

Messiah will proclaim peace (Zech. 9:10-13). At the beginning of World War I, British author H.G. Wells published a book called *The War That Will End War.* On November 11, 1918, at the end of the great war, Prime Minister David Lloyd George said to the British Parliament, "At eleven o'clock this morning came to an end the cruelest and most terrible war that has ever scourged mankind. I hope we may say that thus, this fateful morning, came to an end all wars." But Wells' title proved wrong and Lloyd George's wish was never fulfilled, for war is still with us.

However, when Jesus Christ comes again, He will "speak peace" (v. 10) which means "proclaim peace," for unlike authors and politicians, when Jesus speaks, His words carry authority and things happen (Ps. 33:9). His Word will go forth with power and there will be a general disarmament around the world. Chariots and war horses will be demobilized, every weapon will be destroyed, and "they shall beat their swords into plowshares, and their spears into pruning hooks; nation shall not lift up sword against nation, neither shall they learn war any more" (Isa. 2:4; see Micah 4:3). Our Lord's rule will be universal, from sea to sea and from the Euphrates River to the ends of the earth (see Ps. 72:8).

Zechariah 12:1-9 teaches that there will be one last battle before Jesus establishes His kingdom, as the Gentile armies attack Jerusalem. But the Lord will use Judah as His bow and Ephraim as His arrow and defeat all His enemies (9:13). He will call all His exiled people back from the many nations to which they've been scattered during this age, and they'll return to their "stronghold," which can mean both God their Refuge and the stronghold of Mount Zion. In their land, ruled over by their Messiah, the Jews will receive double blessing in return for all their suffering.

Messiah will march in triumph (9:14–10:1). The image here is that of a storm, not unlike what we read in Psalm 18:7-15 and Habakkuk 3:3-15. Messiah will march forth with a voice like thunder and arrows like lightning, and His army will march with Him. He'll shield them from danger and death and will enable them to defeat their enemies.

In Zechariah 9:15, the image changes from a storm to a feast and the prophet pictures the soldiers shouting like men who are drunk with wine. (See 10:7.) But instead of being drunk on wine, they're "drunk" with the blood of their enemies. Each man is "filled to the brim" like the bowls used at the temple to catch the blood of the sacrifices on the altar (Lev. 4:6-7).

Again, the image changes (Zech. 9:16–10:1) and the army is pictured as a flock of sheep which the Messiah saves by His power. Sheep are the last animals you would take to a war, but Israel has always been God's special flock (Ps. 100:3) and God "the Shepherd of Israel" (80:1). Zechariah will use the "flock" and "shepherd" images again in his prophecy (Zech. 10:2-3; 11:4-16; 13:7).

Once more, the image changes from sheep to precious stones (9:16). When the high priest Joshua was cleansed and clothed, he received the special holy turban that was his crown (3:5), and then he was crowned with a royal diadem that made him king as well as priest (6:9-12). But now it's God's people who are like beautiful precious jewels, sparkling in the land and revealing the beauty of their God.

This section ends with a brief description of the land and the changes God will make for the joy of His people (9:17–10:1). There will be plenty of grain in the fields and fruit in the vineyards because the Lord will provide the rain in its time. How often in their history the Jews turned for help to Baal, the god of storms, instead of turning to the Lord who alone can send the rain. (See 1 Kings 18.) During the Kingdom Age, the land of Palestine will be fruitful and beautiful as God provides the rain that is so necessary for anything to grow.

The promise of rain given in Zechariah 10:1 may have a spiritual meaning behind it, because the Holy Spirit is spoken of in terms of rain (Isa. 32:15; 44:3; Ezek. 29:39; Hosea 6:3; Joel 2:23-32). God promises to pour out His Spirit on Israel (Zech. 12:10) and bring them to repentance and faith in Christ.

Messiah will strengthen His people (10:2-12). Once again the prophet uses the image of the flock, this time a flock led by evil shepherds who cause them to wander and go astray (Matt. 9:36). The Jews were commanded to obey the priests, who would tell them God's will (Ex. 28:30; Lev. 8:8; Ezra 2:63), but too often the leaders turned to diviners and seers and used idolatrous divination devices which were forbidden by the law (Deut. 18:10-12). Israel in the latter days will be like wandering sheep because their leaders will follow lies instead of God's truth (see Ezek. 34).

But Messiah will turn the "sheep" into war-horses! (Zech. 10:3) He will punish the evil shepherds (leaders) and give victory to His people. Several striking images of Messiah are given in verse 4. The *cornerstone* speaks of Christ the foundation for His people, the keystone that joins the walls. (See 3:10 and references to the Stone.) The tent peg refers to Messiah as one on whom burdens may be placed with confidence (see Isa. 22:20-24), and as the battle bow, He is the victorious Warrior who never loses a battle (Ps. 45:5; Isa. 63:2-4). Note that Messiah comes "from Judah" (Zech. 10:4), for God gave the messianic promise to Judah in Genesis 49:10. Every ruler of the nation since David came from the tribe of Judah, for it was with David that God made His covenant (2 Sam. 7).

The emphasis in the rest of the paragraph is on "strength" and "mighty men" (Zech. 10:5-7, 12). Because the Lord will be with the Jews, they will trample their enemies down like mud in the streets, and they will go from victory to victory in the strength of the Lord. God will also call His scattered sheep back home from the many countries where they've been scattered. Just as a shepherd can whistle or play a tune on a pipe and call his flock together, so the Lord will gather His people. It will be like a second "exodus" when they pass through the "sea of affliction" to return to the Lord and to their land.

What a day of victory! God's people Israel will be regathered, redeemed, reunited as one nation, and rejoicing in the strength of the Lord! But this same God can give the same blessings to His church today. We're a scattered people, divided and sometimes distant from each other, but the Lord can unite us in Christ and bring us together. We're fighting battles against the enemy, but the Lord can strengthen us and turn His helpless sheep into victorious war-horses. How much He is willing to do for us, if only we would admit our failures and unbelief and turn to Him for help.

3. Messiah rejected by His people (Zech. 11:1-17)

The two chapters we've just surveyed indicate that Israel will be in trouble in the last days until their Messiah comes to rescue them, cleanse them, and give them a kingdom. How did they get into this trouble?

During the time of David and Solomon, Israel was the

most powerful nation on earth, with wealth and resources beyond measure. After Solomon's death, the nation divided into two kingdoms, Israel and Judah. Israel, the Northern Kingdom, began to deteriorate, so God sent the Assyrians to conquer them and scatter them. Judah had a series of godless kings, so God sent the Babylonians to take Judah captive.

Seventy years later, a small band of Jews returned to their land to rebuild their temple. Life was difficult, and the nation had none of its former glory; but over the years they persisted and restored the temple and the city. Then their Messiah, Jesus Christ, came to them, *and they rejected Him and asked their Roman rulers to have Him crucified.* About forty years later, in A.D. 70, the Roman armies came and destroyed Jerusalem and the temple and scattered the Jews to the nations of the world. Because they didn't receive their own Messiah, they have been a scattered people ever since.

This chapter explains the nation's rejection of the true Messiah and how they will accept a false messiah, the Antichrist, who will appear at the end of the age and deceive the whole world. The key image in the chapter is that of the shepherd, and three different shepherds are presented.

The wailing shepherds (vv. 1-3). These brief verses describe the invasion of the Holy Land by the Romans. Key places like the Jordan, Lebanon, and Bashan are mentioned. The invading army is like a fire that burns the forests. The "wailing shepherds" are the rulers of the nation who have led the people astray and are now paying for their sins. In the East, leaders and rulers were called "shepherds" because they led the people, protected them, and provided for them. Jeremiah saw a similar scene: "Weep and wail, you shepherds; roll in the dust, you leaders of the flock. For your time to be slaughtered has come" (Jer. 25:34, NIV). Usually the shepherds gave the sheep for slaughter, but here the shepherds themselves are led to the slaughter!

The high priest Caiaphas thought that by killing Jesus, he would save the Jewish nation from destruction (John 11:47-53), but just the opposite occurred. By rejecting their Messiah, they opened the doors to judgment and dispersal. It was true that Jesus did die for the nation of Israel, for He died for the sins of the whole world (1 John 2:1-3), but their rejection of truth led to their acceptance of lies, and the result was the Roman invasion and the destruction of their temple and city.

The true Shepherd (Zech. 11:4-14). God commanded Zechariah to play the role of the true Shepherd. He became a type of the Messiah at the time when our Lord was ministering on earth. The flock of Israel was destined for slaughter because of their wicked rulers, but he was to do his best to rescue them. The Jewish leaders weren't concerned about the sheep; they were concerned only about their own position and power. Did Zechariah actually obtain a flock and become a shepherd, or was this only to be written in his book? Isaiah, Jeremiah, and especially Ezekiel used "action sermons" to get the attention of the careless people,[5] so perhaps that's what Zechariah did. He carried the two instruments of a faithful shepherd, a staff (crook) to guide the sheep and a rod to ward off enemies, and he paid special attention to the oppressed ("poor") in the flock, those who needed special attention. According to verse 11, some of the "poor of the flock" were watching him, so apparently this was an "action sermon."

He called the one staff "Beauty" (Favor, Grace) and the other one "Bands" (Union). He fed the flock and even got rid of three unfaithful shepherds. [6] Then one day he broke both of the staves! God's favor to His people had come to an end; the covenant union between God and His people was broken. But so also was the union between Judah (the Southern

Kingdom) and Israel (v. 14).[7]

God is long-suffering and waits for sinners to repent and believe, but there comes a time when He has done all that He will do to reach them. This happened to Israel when Jesus was ministering on earth. "But although He had done so many signs before them, they did not believe in Him" (John 12:37, NKJV). Jesus Himself said, "How often I wanted to gather your children together, as a hen gathers her chicks under her wings, but you were not willing" (Matt. 23:37).

Actually, the people *wanted* Zechariah to quit! He asked for his wages and they gave him the price of a slave, thirty pieces of silver (Ex. 21:32), an amount that he sarcastically called "a lordly—handsome—price." So disgusted was he with his wages that he went to the temple and threw the money to the potter who was working there, perhaps supplying vessels for the priests.

According to Matthew 27:1-10, Zechariah's actions were prophetic, for Judas sold Jesus for thirty pieces of silver, brought the money back, and threw it into the temple. The priests took the money and used it to buy an abandoned potter's field as a cemetery for strangers. But verse 9 attributes the quotation to *Jeremiah,* not Zechariah, a fact that has puzzled Bible students for centuries.

If we have a high view of inspiration, we can't simply dismiss this statement as a mistake or a scribal error; nor can we escape by saying that Jeremiah *spoke* the prophecy, but Zechariah *wrote* it in his book. Wouldn't you expect to find it in Jeremiah's book? Perhaps the solution lies in understanding the way ancient authors used texts from other writers.

First of all, how does Jeremiah get into the picture? It appears that Matthew alludes to Jeremiah's actions recorded in Jeremiah 19, when he broke the jar and pronounced judgment on Judah and Jerusalem. He announced that the Valley of the Son of Hinnom, outside Jerusalem, would become a cemetery because of the sins of the people (Jer. 19:11). Note that this event took place near the entrance of the east gate, which was the Potter's Gate leading to a potter's field (vv. 1-2), and note also the phrase "innocent blood" in verse 4, a phrase that Judas used when he returned the silver to the priests (Matt. 27:4). So, from Jeremiah, Matthew borrowed the images of a potter's field, innocent blood, and a cemetery.

Matthew cited Zechariah 11:12-13 concerning the thirty pieces of silver which were thrown down to the potter in the temple. Why would a potter be in the temple? Since the priests used many different kinds of vessels, the services of a potter would certainly be necessary. So, from Zechariah, Matthew borrowed the temple, the thirty pieces of silver which were thrown down in the temple, and the potter to whom they were thrown.

Now, it's obvious that Zechariah's words don't perfectly parallel the events described in Matthew 27:1-10. In Zechariah, the money was given to the prophet while in Matthew, it was given to Judas the traitor. The prophet gave the money to the potter in the temple, but Judas gave his wages to the priests who then bought a potter's field. What Matthew did was unite (the technical word is "conflate") elements from both Jeremiah and Zechariah, but since Zechariah was a minor prophet, he named only Jeremiah, the major prophet.[8]

Whatever view you take of this matter, it's remarkable that Jesus was sold for thirty pieces of silver, that the silver was thrown down in the temple, and that the silver was used to buy a potter's field. And all of this happened because the Jewish people rejected Zechariah the shepherd and Jesus the Good Shepherd!

The false shepherd (Zech. 11:15-17). The prophet was then commanded to adopt the role of a "foolish shepherd." The word "foolish" doesn't mean "stupid" but "morally deficient, corrupt" because he doesn't receive God's truth. He's also called "a worthless (idle) shepherd," because he doesn't care for the sheep. Unlike the Good Shepherd, he doesn't seek the lost, care for the young, feed the flock, or heal the injured. All he does is slaughter the flock to feed himself! (See Ezek. 34.)

Because Israel rejected their true Shepherd, Jesus Christ, they will one day blindly accept and obey the false shepherd (Antichrist) who will lead them astray. Those who reject the light inevitably accept the darkness. "I have come in My Father's name," said Jesus, "and you do not receive Me; if another comes in his own name, him you will receive" (John 5:43, NKJV).

According to Daniel 9:27, the Antichrist will actually be able to make a covenant with the Jews for seven years. Probably this is for the purpose of protecting them so they can rebuild their temple and resume their sacrifices. But after three and a half years, he'll break the covenant, put his own image in the temple, and force the world to worship him (2 Thes. 2:1-12; Rev. 13).

That God's chosen people, who possess the inspired Scriptures, should reject Him who is "the truth" (John 14:6) and came from the Father, and follow one who is a liar and is energized by Satan, is incredible to comprehend, but it will happen just as the Scripture says. However, the Lord will judge this false shepherd by breaking his power (his right arm) and confusing his mind (right eye), and then Messiah will come from heaven and confine him to the lake of fire for a thousand years (Rev. 19:11-21).

During that thousand years, Christ will reign in His glorious kingdom, Israel will receive the blessings promised by the prophets, the church will reign with Him, and all creation will enter into "the glorious liberty of the children of God"

(Rom. 8:21, NKJV).

Thy kingdom come!

Redeemed, Refined, and Restored

In this second oracle, Zechariah takes us to the end times. He describes the Gentile nations attacking Jerusalem, the Jews experiencing severe trials ("the time of Jacob's trouble"), and then the Lord returning in power and great glory to deliver His people and establish the promised kingdom. What an exciting scenario it is! But it isn't fiction; it's God's own Word, and it will come to pass.

As you study these three chapters, note the repetition of the phrase "in that day," which is found sixteen times. "That day" is "the Day of the Lord," the day of wrath and judgment that the prophets wrote about (Joel 3:9-16; Zeph. 1), and that Jesus described in Matthew 24:4-31 and John in Revelation 6–19.

Zechariah describes three key events.

1. The Lord will deliver Jerusalem (Zech. 12:1-9; 14:1-7)

Jerusalem is mentioned fifty-two times in the Book of Zechariah, and twenty-two of these references are in the final three chapters. In the first chapter of his prophecy, Zechariah told us that God was "jealous for Jerusalem and for Zion with a great jealousy" (1:14). This statement reveals the yearning heart of a loving Father for His firstborn (Ex. 4:22) and the desire of a faithful Husband for His unfaithful bride (Jer. 2:2; 3:2). God's timing isn't always what we would have planned, but He is wiser than we are and will keep His promises to Israel.

Jerusalem will be attacked (Zech. 12:1-3; 14:1-2). The oracle opens with an affirmation of God's sovereignty and power. If we look above us, we see the heavens He created; if we look beneath us, we see the earth that He founded; and if we look within, we find the spirit that He formed. The God of creation is the God who cares for us! "Great is our Lord and mighty in power; His understanding is infinite. The Lord lifts up the humble; He casts the wicked down to the ground" (Ps. 147:5-6, NKJV).

Note the emphasis on "all nations" and "all peoples" (Zech. 12:2-3, 6, 9; 14:2, 12, 14, 16), for this attack involves the armies of the whole world and is part of the famous "battle of Armageddon" described in Joel 3:9-16; Matthew 24:27-30; and Revelation 9:13-18; 16:12-16; and 19:17-21.[1] Three forces are involved in the gathering of this great army: (1) the nations agree to cooperate in their fight against God and His people (Ps. 2:1-3); (2) Satan uses demonic powers to influence the nations to gather (Rev. 16:13-15); and (3) the Lord exercises His sovereign powers in gathering them (Zech. 14:2; Rev. 16:16).

To describe Jerusalem's situation "in that day," Zechariah used the images of a cup and a stone. A cup is a familiar biblical image for judgment (Ps. 75:8; Isa. 51:17, 21-23; Jer. 25:15-28; Ezek. 23:31-33; Hab. 2:16; Rev. 14:10; 16:19; 18:6). The nations plan to "swallow up" Jerusalem, but when they begin to "drink the cup," its contents makes them sick and drunk! History shows that every nation that has ever tried to destroy the Jews has itself been destroyed. It will be no different when the nations collectively attack God's chosen people.

Some of the enemy soldiers will enter the city, loot it, abuse the women, and take half of the inhabitants captive. But the Gentiles' hopes of destroying the city and the nation will be disappointed, for the Lord will make Jerusalem like an immovable rock that won't yield. This stone will eventually cut the invading armies to pieces.

The Lord will visibly appear (Zech. 14:3-7). Our Lord ascended to heaven from the Mount of Olives (Acts 1:9-12), and when He returns to earth, He will stand on the Mount of Olives and cause a great earthquake to change the terrain (Isa. 29:6; Rev. 16:18-19). This will create a new valley that will provide an escape route for many of the people. There will also be changes in the heavens so that the day will be neither light nor darkness, morning nor evening (see Isa. 60:19-20).

"The Lord is a man of war," sang the Jews after they were delivered from Egypt (Ex. 15:3), but this aspect of Christ's character and ministry is ignored, if not opposed, by people today. In their quest for world peace, some denominations have removed the "militant songs" from their hymnals, so that a new generation is growing up knowing nothing about "fighting the good fight of faith" or worshiping a Savior who will one day meet the nations of the world in battle (Rev. 19:11-21).

Before the nation entered the Promised Land, Moses promised them that the Lord would fight for them (Deut. 1:30; 3:22). "Who is the King of glory?" asked David; and his answer was, "The Lord strong and mighty, the Lord mighty in battle" (Ps. 24:8). Isaiah announced, "The Lord will march out like a mighty man, like a warrior He will stir up His zeal; with a shout He will raise the battle cry and will triumph over His enemies" (Isa. 42:13, NIV). Our God has been long-suffering toward the nations, but one day He will meet them in battle and triumph over them.

The Lord will defeat the enemy (Zech. 12:4-9; 14:12-15). Panic, a plague, and special power given to the Jewish warriors (12:8) are the means God will use to conquer the invading armies. The horses will panic in their blindness and the riders will be possessed by madness and end up fighting each other (14:13).[2] God will watch over His people and see to it that they are delivered. He will make the Jews to be like fire and their enemies like dry stubble. Jesus Christ will demonstrate His great power as He defends His people and defeats His enemies.

While the inhabitants of Jerusalem are central in this account, special notice is given to the part Judah will play in the battle. For the invaders to get to Jerusalem, they must march through Judah (12:2); but the Lord will keep watch over the people of Judah and deliver them for David's sake (vv. 4, 7). The faith and courage of the people in Jerusalem will encourage Judah to wax valiant in the fight, and God will enable them to conquer (vv. 5-6). The weakest Jewish warrior will have the power of David, who slew tens of thousands of enemy soldiers (1 Sam. 18:7). The Jewish army will go forth like the Angel of the Lord who slew 185,000 Assyrian soldiers in one night (Isa. 37).

2. The Lord will cleanse Israel (Zech. 12:10-13:9)

In delivering Israel from her enemies, our Lord's ultimate goal is more than their national preservation, for their spiritual restoration is uppermost in His heart. He wants to reveal Himself to them and establish the kind of relationship that was impossible in previous centuries because of their unbelief.

The people will repent (12:10-14). Repentance isn't something we work up ourselves; it's a gift from God as we hear

His Word and recognize His grace (Acts 5:31; 11:18; 2 Tim. 2:25). God will pour out the Spirit[3] upon Israel (Joel 2:28-29), and the people will realize their sins and call out to God for forgiveness. They will also see their Messiah whom the nation pierced (Ps. 22:16; Isa. 53:5; John 19:34, 37) and will put their faith in Him. Forgiveness comes to any believing sinner only through faith in the sacrifice of Christ on the cross.

The nation will go into mourning, the way parents would mourn over the loss of their only son, the way the nation mourned near Megiddo when their beloved King Josiah was slain in battle (2 Chron. 35:20-27). Zechariah mentions that all the families (clans) of Israel will mourn, the men and women separately, and this will include royalty (David's clan), the prophets (Nathan's clan; see 2 Sam. 7), and the priests (Levi's and Shimei's clans; Num. 3:17-18, 21). "All the families that remain" covers the rest of the nation. It will be a time of deep and sincere national repentance such as has not been seen before.

The nation will be cleansed (Zech. 13:1-7). Isaiah had admonished the nation, "Wash yourselves, make yourselves clean; put away the evil of your doings from before My eyes" (Isa. 1:16, NKJV), but they refused to listen. Jeremiah had pleaded with his people, "O Jerusalem, wash your heart from wickedness, that you may be saved" (Jer. 4:14, NKJV), but they wouldn't obey. But now, in response to Israel's repentance and faith, the Lord will wash them clean! This forgiveness is part of the new covenant that God promised to His people (Jer. 31:31-34): "For I will forgive their wickedness and will remember their sins no more" (v. 34).

William Cowper based his hymn "There Is a Fountain Filled with Blood" on Zechariah 13:1, for it's the sacrifice of Christ that atones for sin. The Jews could cleanse their external ceremonial uncleanness by washing in water, but for internal cleansing the sinful heart of men and women can be cleansed only by the blood of the Savior (Lev. 16:30; 17:11). "And He Himself is the propitiation for our sins, and not for ours only but also for the whole world" (1 John 2:2, NKJV).

But not only will their hearts be cleansed, but the land itself will be purged of all that is deceitful and defiling. The idols and the false prophets[4]—two of Israel's besetting sins—will be removed, as well as the very "unclean spirit" that caused people to turn from God. (See Zech. 5:5-11.)

According to the Law, false prophets were to be killed (Deut. 13); so the false prophets in that day will lie about their occupation in order to save their lives (13:2-6). They won't wear their special garments (v. 4; 2 Kings 1:8; Matt. 3:4), and they'll claim to be farmers rather than prophets. If asked about the scars on their bodies, actually caused by wounds inflicted while worshiping idols (1 Kings 18:28), they will lie and claim that their friends (or family) inflicted the wounds to discipline them. [5]

In contrast to the false prophets, the true Shepherd is presented in Zechariah 13:7. (Review Zech. 11 for the other "Shepherd" prophecies.) Jesus quoted part of this prophecy when He was on His way to Gethsemane with His disciples (Matt. 26:31), and He referred to it again when He was arrested in the garden (v. 56). Only Jesus the Messiah could the Father call "the man who is My fellow," that is, "the man who is My equal." (See John 10:30 and 14:9.)

But there is also a wider meaning of this text as it relates to the scattering of the nation in A.D. 70 when Jerusalem was taken by the Romans. The Jews had smitten their Shepherd on the cross (Isa. 53:10), and this act of rejection led to the nation being scattered (Deut. 28:64; 29:24-25). Israel today is a dispersed people, but one day they shall be gathered; they are a defiled people, but one day they shall be cleansed.

The nation will be refined (Zech. 13:8-9). This image

reminds us of the value God puts on His people Israel: they are like gold and silver that need to be refined in the furnace of affliction. This had been their experience in Egypt (Deut. 4:20) and in Babylon (Isa. 48:10), but "the time of Jacob's trouble" will be their most difficult "furnace experience."

The goldsmith refines the gold or silver so that the dross may be removed, and that's what the Tribulation in the last days will accomplish for Israel. One third of the people will be spared, the true believing remnant, while the rest will be rejected and perish. That godly remnant who called on the Lord (Acts 2:21) will be saved and become the nucleus of the promised kingdom, for the Lord will acknowledge them as His own people (see Hosea 2:21-23).

Before we leave this section, we need to see the spiritual application for God's people today. Certainly the church is a defiled people who need to repent and be cleansed, and the promise of forgiveness is still valid (1 John 1:9). God often has to put us through the furnace of suffering before we'll call on Him and seek His face (Heb. 12:3-11; 1 Peter 4:12). If God's people will follow the instructions of 2 Chronicles 7:14, the Lord will cleanse and bless the church and bring healing to the land.

3. The Lord reigns over all the earth (Zech. 14:8-11, 16-21)

"And the Lord shall be king over all the earth; in that day shall there be one Lord, and His name one" (v. 9). After the nations have been punished and Israel has been purified, the Lord will establish His righteous kingdom and reign on David's throne (Luke 1:32-33; Rev. 17:14; 19:16). His reign will be universal ("over all the earth"), He will be the only God worshiped, and His name will be the only name honored. (See Ps. 72; Jer. 30:7-9.) What will happen when the King reigns supremely?

The land will be healed (Zech. 14:8). Jerusalem is the only great city of antiquity that wasn't built near a large river. But during the Kingdom Age,[6] a river of "living waters" will flow from Jerusalem and bring healing and fertility to the land. (See Ezek. 47:1-12 and Joel 3:18.) The river will divide so the waters can flow to the Dead Sea ("former sea," KJV, "eastern sea," NIV) and to the Mediterranean Sea ("hinder," KJV, "western," NIV). For centuries people have been wondering how the Dead Sea could be rescued, but it won't be accomplished until the kingdom. For a beautiful description of the land during the Kingdom Age, read Isaiah 35.

The topography will be changed (Zech. 14:10-11). Besides the changes caused by the earthquake at Christ's return (vv. 4-5), two other changes will occur: (1) the land around Jerusalem will be lowered and leveled and become a plain, and (2) Jerusalem itself will be raised above the land around it. These changes will be the fulfillment of Isaiah's prophecy, "Now it shall come to pass in the latter days that the mountain of the Lord's house shall be established on the top of the mountains, and shall be exalted above the hills; and all nations shall flow to it" (Isa. 2:2, NKJV; and see Zech. 8:1-3 and Micah 4:1-3).

If Messiah is to reign as King-Priest (Zech. 6:9-15), then there must be a temple and a priesthood during the Kingdom Age, and it is described in detail in Ezekiel 40–48. Jerusalem will be the most important city on earth and the temple area the most important part of that glorious new city.[7]

All dangers will be removed (Zech. 14:11). The mountains round about Jerusalem were for her protection (Pss. 48:1-8; 125:1-2); but now that Messiah is reigning, the city no longer faces danger from enemy invasion (Ezek. 34:22-31). "It will be inhabited" (NIV) reminds us that only 50,000 Jews were willing to leave the safe and comfortable city of Babylon to live in the ruins of Jerusalem, and even Nehemiah had trouble getting people to live in the city (Neh. 11). Zechariah has already told us that the children will play in the streets, and the old men and women will sit in the sun and talk together (Zech. 8:4-8).

The Gentiles will worship at Jerusalem (14:16). Israel will have a ministry to the Gentiles who will trust the true and living God and come to Jerusalem to worship at His temple (Isa. 2:2-5; Zech. 2:10-13). Of the seven annual feasts listed in Leviticus 23, the Feast of Tabernacles is the only one that will be celebrated during the Kingdom Age (Lev. 23:33-44). This feast commemorated the nation's wilderness wanderings, but it also was a time of rejoicing at the bountiful blessings of the Lord during the harvest (v. 40).

But why celebrate only the Feast of Tabernacles? Merrill Unger makes an excellent suggestion when he points out that the Feast of Tabernacles is the only one of the seven feasts of Leviticus 23 that will not have been fulfilled when the kingdom is established.

Passover was fulfilled in the death of Christ (1 Cor. 5:7; John 1:29), Firstfruits in His resurrection (15:23), and the week-long Feast of Unleavened Bread in the life of the church today as believers walk in holiness (5:6-8). Pentecost was fulfilled in Acts 2, and the Feast of Trumpets will be fulfilled before the kingdom begins when God regathers His people from the ends of the earth (Isa. 18:3, 7; Matt. 24:29-31). The Day of Atonement will be fulfilled when the nation sees her Messiah, repents, and is cleansed.

But the Feast of Tabernacles foreshadows the joyful and fruitful Kingdom Age, so it will be celebrated while the kingdom is in progress.[8] It will be an annual reminder to the Gentile nations that the bountiful blessings they enjoy come from a gracious and generous Lord. How easy it is to take our blessings for granted!

The Lord will exercise justice (Zech. 14:17-19). The nations that don't send their representatives to Jerusalem to worship will be disciplined by getting no rain for their land. This is the way God disciplined Israel when she refused to obey Him (Deut. 28:22-24). Remember, though the millennium is a time of peace and blessing, it is also a time when Jesus will reign over all the earth "with a rod of iron" and will judge disobedience (Ps. 2:9; Rev. 2:27; 12:5; 19:15). Not to celebrate the Feast of Tabernacles would be tantamount to despising the blessings of the Lord, and this is a serious transgression. (See Rom. 1:18.)

Egypt is mentioned specifically because that nation especially depended on the annual flooding of the Nile for irrigation, and without the rains, the river could not rise. During the time of Joseph, there were seven years of terrible famine in Egypt. Also, Egypt had been Israel's persecutor and enemy, and during the kingdom, she will enjoy blessing because of Israel's Messiah. Not to show gratitude would be a heinous sin.

Holiness will characterize all of life (Zech. 14:20-21). We might expect "holiness" to be written on the bells of the high priest's robe (Ex. 28:36-38), but certainly not on the bells worn by the horses! And why would the common utensils in the home be treated like vessels used in the temple?[9] These two images are God's way of saying, "In the Kingdom Age every aspect of life will be holy to the Lord." God had called Israel to be "a kingdom of priests" (Ex. 19:6), and now they would be just that by God's grace.

For the believer today, this is the Old Testament version of 1 Corinthains 10:31, "Therefore, whether you eat or drink, or whatever you do, do all to the glory of God" (NKJV). There is no "secular" or "sacred" in the Christian life, because everything comes from God and should be used for His glory.

The Hebrew word translated "Canaanite" in Zechariah

14:21 refers to merchants and traders or to any unclean person, both of whom would defile the temple of God. When Jesus began His ministry and ended it, He found "religious merchants" using God's house for personal gain (John 2:13-22; Matt. 21:12-13; Mark 11:15-17; Luke 19:45-46). The house of prayer for all nations had been turned into a den of thieves for the profit of the Jewish high priest and his family. But the millennial temple will be a holy temple, not defiled by those who neither know the Lord nor love Him, and in it a holy priesthood will serve the Lord.

Zechariah's book begins with a call to repentance, but it ends with a vision of a holy nation and a glorious kingdom. Zechariah was one of God's heroes who ministered at a difficult time and in a difficult place, but he encouraged God's people by showing them visions of what God has planned for their future. God is still jealous over Jerusalem and the Jewish people, and He will fulfill His promises.

"Pray for the peace of Jerusalem" (Ps. 122:6).

Wanted: Holy Heroes and Heroines

> In the world's broad field of battle,
> In the bivouac of life,
> Be not like dumb, driven cattle!
> Be a hero in the strife!

Henry Wadsworth Longfellow wrote those words in his familiar poem "A Psalm of Life." Someone has adapted Longfellow's poem for the church today:

> In the world's broad field of battle,
> In the bivouac of life,
> You will find the Christian soldier
> Represented by his wife.

Without denying that some men do leave the spiritual heroics to their wives, I confess that I don't totally agree with that cynical paraphrase. During nearly fifty years of ministry in many parts of the world, I've met too many Christian men who, with their wives and children, are living heroically to the glory of God. Heroism isn't a matter of gender. Church history records the stories of both women and men who qualify to be called "Heroes of Faith," and we won't get the stories of the millions of anonymous heroes until we get to heaven. God knows who they are and that's all that really matters.

Four decades ago, American historian Arthur M. Schlesinger, Jr., published an essay entitled "The Decline of Heroes" in which he blames modern society for the absence of heroes, the kind of men and women who "seized history with both hands and gave it an imprint, even a direction, which it otherwise might not have had."[1] According to Schlesinger, today's society emphasizes "collectivism," not individuality, with everybody comfortably merging into a group and enjoying the comfort of conformity. This doesn't leave much room for the courageous and even eccentric man or woman who has a vision and dares to be different. "Where does the great man [or woman] fit into our homogenized society?" he asks.[2] Many people aren't too comfortable with heroes; they show the rest of us how small we really are.

Thanks to modern media, artificial "heroes," both secular and sacred, can be manufactured almost overnight. "Two centuries ago when a great man appeared," writes Samuel Boorstin, "people looked for God's purpose in him; today we look for his press agent."[3] Alas, today's church has more than its share of manufactured heroes; but it also has many true heroes who serve God and His people with humility and courage. The problem is, we need more heroes in the church if we're to fulfill the challenges God's put before us.

As we review the three Old Testament books we've studied, what can we conclude about God's heroes?

1. God's heroes come in many sizes and shapes. There is no set pattern. Ezra was a well-educated priest who knew the Law of God and could teach it. Haggai was an old man who thought more like the younger generation, and Zechariah was a young man on whom God placed the heavy burden of prophecy. Zerubbabel had royal blood in his veins, but he willingly served as an administrator under the Persian government. Joshua, the high priest, lived among the people and tried to encourage them. And, working with these men were many devoted men and women, unnamed in Scripture but known to God, who daily carried burdens, faithfully did their work, and sought to be builders instead of wreckers.

The world gives us a stereotyped picture of what successful leaders are like, but there is no set pattern, whether in business, government, or the church. In fact, not all of God's heroes are necessarily "leaders"; many are simply obedient followers. The important thing is that, like Ezra, we have God's good hand upon us, and like Joshua and Zerubbabel, we experience the oil of God's Spirit empowering us.

I've been privileged to serve on the boards of several ministries, and from this experience I've learned this: God is sovereign in training and calling His servants, and it's often the "maverick" who doesn't seem to belong who sees the Lord do exceptional things. God's heroes aren't carbon copies; they're originals. They dare to be themselves and do the work God's called them to do.

2. God's heroes see opportunities, but don't ignore the problems. The 50,000 Jews who went to Judah to rebuild the temple knew that life wouldn't be as easy in Jerusalem as it was in Babylon, but they also knew that there was a job to be done. Ezra could have stayed in Babylon and established a successful Bible school, but he chose to change his classification from "settler" to "pioneer" and move to Jerusalem. Did he know about the obstacles and problems he would face? Of course, but he preferred to look at the opportunities.

We seem to forget that the thing that kept the "heroes of the faith" going, such as the people listed in Hebrews 11, was their vision of God and what He wanted them to do. Abraham saw the city of God and therefore wasn't tempted by Egypt or Sodom as Lot was (Heb. 11:13-16). Moses saw "Him who is invisible" and the reward God has for the faithful, so he rejected the treasure and pleasure of Egypt and identified with the suffering people of God (Heb. 11:24-27).

God's heroes are captivated by God, who He is, what He does, and what He wants them to do. When you look at their eyes, you see a faraway expression that means they've caught the vision. In too many churches today, the leaders are content to monitor conformity, and the church is a parking lot, not a launching pad. There's no vision because people are looking back instead of ahead.

3. God's heroes trust the promises of God's Word. "And they prospered through the prophesying of Haggai, the prophet, and Zechariah, the son of Iddo" (Ezra 6:14). If you ignore the Word of God, you'll become "visionary" instead of a person of vision. No amount of personal charisma, vocational training, or ministry experience can substitute for believing God's promises and acting upon them.

Haggai's messages got the people off dead center and back to the work of rebuilding the temple. Zechariah assured them of God's personal concern for His people and that He had a glorious future planned for them. Through the prophets, God encouraged Zerubbabel to finish the work, and Joshua to continue representing the people before Jehovah.

God's heroes spend time fellowshipping with God and meditating on His Word (Josh. 1:8; Ps. 1:1-3). They can face any enemy because they know and trust the promises of God.

4. God's heroes know how to work together. In spite of the fact that heroes are sometimes individualists and even eccentrics, they know they can't do the work alone. The isolated ministry is destined to become a terminated ministry, because God's people belong to each other, affect each other, and need each other.

The Apostle Paul was perhaps the greatest theologian-missionary who ever lived, yet he didn't attempt to serve the Lord in isolation. At his side were people like Luke, Timothy, Barnabas, John Mark, Titus, Epaphroditus, Euodia and Syntyche, and a host of others, including the twenty-six people named in Romans 16. He brought out the greatness in them and they helped him bear the burdens of ministry. They all needed each other.

Ezra was a brilliant scribe, a gifted teacher of the Law, yet he was willing to work alongside people who didn't have that kind of training. Haggai was an old man who had seen Solomon's temple, and Zechariah was a young man, born in Babylon, yet they ministered together and served the Lord. God's heroes look beyond gender, age, education, and experience and only ask, "Is the good hand of God upon you? Is the oil of God on your life and ministry?"

5. God's heroes aren't afraid of change. A friend asked me one day, "Do you know how many church officers it takes to change a light bulb?" When I confessed I didn't know, he replied, "Change!" and we both laughed.

But the subject of change in the church is more than grist for the humor mill; it's one of the keys to the future ministry of our churches. Of course, some things (like doctrine) must never change, but some things have to change or we'll find ourselves isolated from the people we claim we're reaching.

Young Zechariah dared to announce that the traditional fasts should be replaced by feasts. That must have shaken the traditionalists back in Babylon. And he even went so far as to set a crown on the head of Joshua the high priest! I can imagine some of the Jewish elders in Jerusalem saying to each other, "We've got to do something about these young prophets! That's what happens when you don't graduate from the right schools." But what Zechariah did honored the Lord and pointed to the coming of the Priest-King Jesus Christ.

6. God's heroes expect opposition, but they also expect God to help them overcome it. Paul wrote to his friends in Corinth: "But I will tarry in Ephesus until Pentecost. For a great and effective door has opened to me, and there are many adversaries" (1 Cor. 16:8-9, NKJV). We would expect him to say that he was staying in Ephesus because things were going so well and there were no adversaries, but it was just the opposite. Opportunities always arouse adversaries, but adversaries have a way of providing more opportunities.

God's heroes don't pack up and leave just because somebody is opposing them and their work. That's the difference between the true shepherd and the hireling (John 10:1-5). The shepherd is there for the sake of the sheep, not the salary, and the presence of trouble only makes him more diligent. Shepherds expect wolves to attack the sheep and they prepare for it.

The early church expected opposition and let God take care of it. Their greatest concern wasn't their comfort or even their safety; it was their ministry. They didn't pray for escape; they prayed for enablement. "Now, Lord, consider their threats and enable your servants to speak Your word with great boldness" (Acts 4:29, NIV). That's the way God's heroes pray, a good example for us to follow today.

7. God's heroes are concerned about future generations. When God rebuked King Hezekiah for his folly and told him that the treasures he'd boasted about would one day be carried to Babylon, the king's response was, "At least there will be peace and truth in my days" (Isa. 39). What a shortsighted view of life and ministry! As long as I'm safe and comfortable, why worry about future generations?

The people we met in our studies were concerned about the spiritual opportunities available for their children and grandchildren. They wanted future generations to have a temple in which to worship and the Word of God to study and obey. Yes, the past generations had failed the Lord and God had to destroy their temple and city. But that was no reason for the new generation to quit and let Jerusalem and the temple lie in ruins. "If the foundations be destroyed, what can the righteous do?" (Ps. 11:3) *They can lay new foundations and rebuild!*

When Joshua's generation and the generation following passed off the scene, the nation of Israel turned away from the Lord and began to serve idols (Jud. 2:6-15). Ancient history? No, present reality, for every local church is but one generation short of extinction. If we don't reach our own children and grandchildren for the Lord today, there may be no church tomorrow.

God's heroes take the long view of life; they see the big picture. They feel keenly the responsibility laid down in 2 Timothy 2:2—"And the things that you have heard from me among many witnesses, commit these to faithful men who will be able to teach others also" (NKJV). Paul—Timothy—faithful men—others also: that's four generations of believers! But suppose Timothy didn't obey, or the faithful men weren't really faithful? What would happen to the "others"?

8. God's heroes have a courage that comes from a close walk with God. No matter what talents or abilities we may possess by God's grace, if we don't have the courage to use them, we might as well not have them. Have you ever tried to steer a car when it's in neutral? It can't be done. You have to put in the key, get the motor running, and put the car in gear before you can travel.

Too many people are living with their spiritual gears in neutral. They're afraid to do anything for fear they'll get hurt, do something wrong, or make a mess of everything. They occasionally rev up the motor just to encourage themselves, forgetting that the sound of power isn't the same as putting that power to work and going somewhere.

"Be on guard. Stand true to what you believe. Be courageous. Be strong." That's the way *The New Living Translation* translates 1 Corinthians 16:13. These are good admonitions for would-be heroes. It isn't enough to know what I believe and to guard it. I've got to put my faith to work, and that takes courage. An Italian proverb says, "It's better to live one day as a lion than a hundred years as a sheep." But God's people don't have to choose between meekness and courage; we can exercise both and not be inconsistent. After all, isn't our Savior both the Lion and the Lamb? (Rev. 5:5-6)

God is still searching for all kinds of men and women who will be "holy heroes" in a world that lies in ruins because of sin. They won't all be put into prominent places like Ezra and Joshua and Zerubbabel, but every place is an important place in the plan of God, if we're doing the will of God.

Are you ready to be heroic for the Lord?

Chapter One

The Providence of God
(Ezra 1–3)

1. What characteristics or actions qualify the returning Jewish exiles to be considered heroes?

2. What difficult God-given challenges can you now give thanks for? How did you grow through them?

3. If a nonbeliever were to point out some of the number of "inconsistencies" in Ezra as evidence of error in the Bible, how would you answer?

4. Think of a current political leader in your country. How might God be using him or her to accomplish God's purposes at this time?

5. What application can you make from the fact that God "stirred the spirit of Cyrus" and "stirred the hearts of the Jews" to accomplish His will? Have you ever had your heart "stirred"?

6. How do you assess the statement, "a decay in the quality of a nation's leaders is an indication that trouble is ahead"? How would you rate your country in this regard?

7. Why were genealogies and record-keeping so important to the Jews?

8. What analogies can you draw for the Christian life as you read about the extensive preparation and work to lay the foundation of the temple?

9. Wiersbe stated about the Jews, "Their tasks were varied, but they all had one goal before them." What is the goal (or goals) that the church is working toward today? Why is unity essential in this work?

10. In what way can the past be a "rudder to guide us"?

How can you avoid having the past be "an anchor to hold (you) back"?

Chapter Two

The Faithfulness of God
(Ezra 4–6)

1. In what ways have you been reminded that God is faithful? How can you remind others of this truth?

2. What does this statement mean: "God's commandments are God's enablements"?

3. Where in your life or your church have you seen opportunity and opposition paired together?

4. What are symptoms of religious confusion in your society today?

5. What is the difference between separation and isolation? How would this apply in the areas of marriage, friendship, school, work, and neighborhood?

6. What has discouraged you the most in your walk or work for the Lord? How do you counteract this?

7. What means did God use to help the Jews overcome obstacles and apathy toward their rebuilding task?

8. Which figure in church history inspires you the most as one that God used to arouse His people?

9. What should a Christian's relationship be like with local officials and civil authorities?

10. Compared to the Jewish view of their rebuilt temple, how should church buildings be thought of today? How could you show your dedication to the Lord?

C h a p t e r   T h r e e

The Good Hand of God
(Ezra 7-8)

1. If someone asked you the secret of your success in a certain area, how would you answer?

2. What is the relationship between human effort and "the good hand of the Lord" in the development of a success?

3. As you consider the various leaders in your life, what impact for good or ill did they have upon you?

4. How can you make the most of your own family heritage for the kingdom of God?

5. What does it mean that Ezra "set his heart to study the law of the Lord"?

6. Which part of your responsibility with the Word of God comes most easily to you: studying, practicing, obeying, or teaching? Which is the most difficult?

7. Wiersbe comments that Artaxerxes probably didn't have a pure motive in his generosity to the Jews. What difference, if any, does a pure motive make?

8. In what way can you relate to the lack of zeal in the new generation of Jews to get back to Jerusalem?

9. How can you insure that you don't become "too settled" and so resist God's calling to make a move?

10. What journey are you on for which you need reassurance that "Our God is the Alpha and the Omega; what He starts, He finishes"?

Chapter Four

The Grace of God
(Ezra 9-10)

1. What "easier life" might you prefer if it weren't for the call of God upon you?

2. What is the difference between "religious gossip" and honest concern?

3. What was so special about the Jews that to intermarry with the Canaanites would be a defilement?

4. How did Ezra respond when he became aware of the intermarriage sins? What can you learn from this today?

5. When people are no longer appalled by sin, what has happened to them? What is the solution?

6. What personal change would need to occur for you to tremble at God's Word?

7. When have you been, like Ezra, ashamed, embarrassed, and speechless before the Lord?

8. Why didn't the Jews learn their lesson from the chastisements?

9. Wiersbe states that the congregation's conviction of sin "wasn't something that Ezra worked up; it was something that he prayed down." How could this apply to the planning of your worship or revival services?

10. When you read dates translated into our terms such as December 19 and March 27, how does this affect the impact of the passage on you?

C h a p t e r   F i v e

Stirring Up God's People
(Haggai 1)

1. What task have you undertaken with great zeal for the Lord, only later to lose that zeal and grow apathetic?

2. Which of Haggai's four admonitions to the leaders and people do you need to hear the most?

3. How can a person know when the timing is right for a ministry?

4. When, if ever, have you questioned the dependability of the Word of God? How would you help someone who was struggling with this?

5. What guidelines might be useful in determining whether a person was putting too much money and effort into their own dwelling and comfort?

6. How does consideration of priorities fit into your budgeting decisions?

7. God promised to materially bless the Israelites when they were obedient. What relevance or carry-over applies to the church today?

8. What is the relationship between the material and the spiritual?

9. In what way can you give of your best to the Lord? Where are the areas in which you find yourself holding back?

10. What gives you the motivation, will, and strength to obey in spite of the consequences?

Chapter Six

Keeping the Work Alive
(Haggai 2)

1. What are the key phrases in chapter two with which God, through Haggai, encouraged the Israelites? (You may want to check various translations.)

2. What is the role of the Holy Spirit in the Old Testament in general, and in Haggai's time in particular?

3. Read Hebrews 12:25-29. What does this mean to you?

4. Why do you think God's promise of provision was so important to the Jews? In what sense does this promise also comfort you?

5. What was Haggai's point in his questions about the transmission of holiness and defilement?

6. What could be an alternative to the common division of responsibilities in the local church where the elders are assigned the spiritual concerns and the deacons are assigned the material concerns?

7. If Zerubbabel was encouraged to keep on because he was God's special, chosen servant, how could you derive and pass on that same encouragement?

8. What is essential to begin, sustain, and encourage the work of God?

9. What do you think are crucial ingredients for a fruitful ministry carried out by co-laborers?

10. Which of the five practical lessons apply most directly to you today?

Chapter Seven

God and His People
(Zechariah 1 – 2)

1. How did the ministries of Haggai and Zechariah differ from and complement one another?

2. What were the two major emphases Zechariah had as he ministered to the remnant? Why is it important that the people receive both emphases?

3. Who does this promise apply to, "Return to Me . . . and I will return to you"?

4. Why is it important to call people to repentance? How can you do this?

5. In what way do you think the Lord is identifying Himself with the distress of His people today?

6. What were the comforting words the angel brought to Zechariah? How might truly believing these words make a difference in your life?

7. When your circumstances look hopeless, what do you need to be reminded of?

8. What is the significance of the four horns and the four craftsmen in Zechariah's second vision?

9. How can Zechariah 2:1-5 be applied to current events in Israel and/or Jerusalem?

10. What can you learn from the three night visions of Zechariah?

Chapter Eight

God and His Leaders
(Zechariah 3 – 4)

1. When have you seen the work of Satan, the adversary and accuser, at work in your life or the life of someone you know?

2. Of what use is it to go through the fire of trials?

3. What is the meaning of God's words, "Take away the filthy garments from him" and then having him "clothed with the festal robes and a clean turban"? (3:4-5)

4. What must always be involved with cleansing and restoration?

5. How are the priest, the branch, and the stone all images of the coming Messiah?

6. When will the removal of Israel's sins in one day (3:9) occur?

7. What lessons can you draw from the vision of the golden lampstand?

8. How did the verse "Not by might nor by power, but by My Spirit" (4:6) likely affect the Jews as they looked at the task to be done?

9. How can you make sure you are not relying on a "synthetic Pentecost"?

10. What "small things" have you seen God use to accomplish His plan?

C h a p t e r   N i n e

God and the Nations
(Zechariah 5-6)

1. What was the true purpose of the law?

2. How would you rate the state of morality today in our society and in the church?

3. What seems to be the main symptom of wickedness (5:6-11) which God removes?

4. In what ways does the last commandment of "Do Not Covet" relate to the other nine commandments?

5. What does Wiersbe say is the cumulative effect of the vision of chariots and horses?

6. What have you learned about angels as you study Zechariah?

7. What was unexpected about God's instructions concerning the crown?

8. Of what did the crown serve as a reminder? How are you reminded of this same promise?

9. How does the word "diligently" add substance to the condition that the people "diligently obey the Lord your God"?

10. What is the difference between the application and the interpretation of Scriptures?

C h a p t e r   T e n

Truth, Traditions, and Promises
(Zechariah 7–8)

1. What is the role of tradition in your local church body?

2. Where should religious regulations fit into the life of a maturing Christian?

3. What conditions most tempt you to have religion be just a part of your life?

4. Where is the richness found in tradition? What is the danger of tradition?

5. What effect do people's promises have on you? What effect do God's promises have on you?

6. Which part of the future promises of God do you long for the most?

7. What must you remember about material blessings?

8. What obligations did God remind His people of? (vv. 14-19)

9. How specifically can you change your way of living so that others beg you, "Let us go with you, for we have heard that God is with you"?

10. What can you as a Christian believer do for the people of Israel?

Chapter Eleven

Messiah, the Shepherd-King
(Zechariah 9–11)

1. What must you keep in the forefront of your mind as you study complex prophecies?

2. As you watch history unfold, what are you also watching at the same time?

3. What role did the conquests of Alexander the Great play in God's plan?

4. What differences do you see between these two conquerors: Alexander the Great and Jesus the Messiah?

5. When Jesus "speaks peace" (9:10), what will happen?

6. When people don't look to the Shepherd, what other sources do they look to for guidance, comfort, and peace?

7. How can believers take hold of the strength that is promised them from the Lord?

8. Who were the "wailing shepherds" (11:3) and why were they wailing?

9. What message was Zechariah's possible action sermon intended to convey?

10. Why shouldn't Christians dismiss the quote attribution in Matthew 27:9 as a mistake or scribal error?

Chapter Twelve

Redeemed, Refined, and Restored
(Zechariah 12–14)

1. What are the three key events of the end times?

2. What is the significance of describing Jerusalem as a cup and a stone?

3. How do you view the use of militant hymns and teachings on the Lord as a "man of war"?

4. What means will God use to conquer the invading armies?

5. How will the Israelites finally come to repentance?

6. What is the importance of fulfilled prophecy such as in Zechariah 13:7?

7. Based on 2 Chronicles 7:14, how do you envision the "healing" of our land?

8. What does the Feast of the Tabernacles celebrate and how will it be fulfilled?

9. Who will be disciplined in the millennium?

10. For a Christian, what is the relationship of the secular and the sacred?

Chapter Thirteen

Wanted: Holy Heroes and Heroines
(Review)

1. What is a hero?

2. Who have you personally known that you could consider a hero?

3. What are two important factors needed to be a heroic servant for God?

4. What are the eight conclusions Wiersbe makes about heroes?

5. What keeps heroes of the faith going?

6. What promises of God do you trust in as you seek to be a type of hero for God?

7. How can you know when a change is God's will and when it is veering away from God's will?

8. What opposition do you expect in your service for the Lord?

9. What is our responsibility to the next generation of Christians?

10. When do you notice your "spiritual gear in neutral"? How can you make the shift?

NOTES

Preface

1. For a study of Nehemiah, see my book *Be Determined,* also published by ChariotVictor. My exposition on the rest of the Minor Prophets may be found in *Be Amazed* and *Be Concerned,* both published by ChariotVictor.

Chapter 1

1. *My Utmost for His Highest,* July 7.

2. Boorstin, Daniel J. *The Image: A Guide to Pseudo-Events in America* (New York: Harper and Row, 1964), 61.

3. If we calculate from the fall of Jerusalem (587–586) to when the first group of exiles returned (538), we have about fifty years. Perhaps we should see this as another evidence of God's mercy, for He shortened the time of their exile.

4. It may seem strange that not all the Jews elected to go back home, but they had been in Babylon several decades and had settled down to as normal a life as they could have away from their homes and temple. In fact, the Prophet Jeremiah had instructed them to be the best citizens possible (Jer. 29:1-7). Lacking a temple and priesthood, the Jews developed synagogue worship during their captivity; and with the synagogue appeared the body of teachers we know as the scribes and Pharisees. Life in captivity was neither dangerous nor unbearable; and for many of the Jews, the long journey back to Judah was an impossible challenge.

The Book of Esther and the Book of Daniel prove that God had work in Babylon for some of the Jews to do.

5. Is it right for God's people to accept and use for God's work wealth that comes from unbelievers? In one sense, the Babylonians owed this money to the Jews whom they plundered so ruthlessly during their invasion of Judah. The Prophet Haggai (2:8) makes it clear that all wealth belongs

to God and He can distribute it as He sees fit. However, we need to follow the example of Abraham and refuse wealth that would compromise our testimony or put us under obligation to unbelievers (Gen. 14:18-24). Deuteronomy 23:17-18 warns us that money earned from sinful activities is not welcomed by God.

6. "Tirshatha" in the KJV, a Persian word translated "governor" in the NIV and NASB. The same title was given to Nehemiah (Neh. 7:65, 70; 8:9; 10:1). It means "the feared one" and is the equivalent of "Your Excellency" or "Your Reverence" in English. Charles Spurgeon's wife used to call him "the Tirshatha."

7. We aren't told why Joshua the high priest didn't have the Urim and Thummim, as they were an important part of his glorious vestments. During the Babylonian Captivity, the Jews didn't seem to have the special miracles from God that had often accompanied them (Ps. 74:9), although the Prophets Ezekiel and Daniel had wonderful revelations from God. There is no biblical evidence that the use of the Urim and Thummim was restored after the captivity.

8. Maclaren, Alexander. *Expositions of Holy Scripture* (Grand Rapids: Baker Book House, 1974), vol. 1, 77.

9. Ibid., vol. 3, 290.

Chapter 2

1. Tozer, A.W. *The Knowledge of the Holy* (New York: Harper and Brothers, 1961), 85.

2. Taylor, Dr. and Mrs. Howard. *Hudson Taylor's Spiritual Secret* (London: China Inland Mission, 1949), 111.

3. Ezra 4:8–6:18 is written in Aramaic rather than Hebrew, and so is Ezra 7:12-26. These letters and the decree were copied from official documents kept in government archives.

4. Ezra 4:12 is the first place in Scripture where you find the word "Jews." It refers, of course, to the people of Judah.

5. Historians estimate that Artaxerxes I collected between 20 and 35 million dollars annually from his subjects.

6. Spurgeon, Charles. *Metropolitan Tabernacle Pulpit* (Pasadena, Texas: Pilgrim Publications, 1986), vol. 7, 13.

7. When he laid the foundation of the temple, Zerubbabel followed the dimensions given in the Law of Moses, but the edict allowed him to make a bigger structure.

8. The Hebrew word for "dedication" is *hanukkah*, which is the name of the Jewish holiday in December during which they remember the rededication of the temple in 165 B.C. The temple had been taken by the Gentiles and defiled, but the courageous Jews, led by Judas Maccabeus, captured it, cleansed it, and dedicated it to the Lord.

9. That Darius, King of Persia, should be called "king of Assyria" in 6:22 shouldn't disturb us. In Nehemiah 13:6, Artaxerxes, king of Persia, is called "king of Babylon." Darius' kingdom included Assyria, so the title applied.

Chapter 3

1. Of course, God is spirit and doesn't possess literal hands such as we do. The phrase is what theologians call "anthropomorphic," that is, attributing to God something that is true of humans ("anthrop" = human; "morphos" = form). God doesn't have eyes, but He "sees" what's going on in the world; He doesn't have ears, but He "hears" our cries. Because He's a Person, God has the ability to act and respond, and the Bible uses human terminology to explain this. When Isaiah wanted to show the greatness of God, he said that God measured the waters "in the hollow of His hand" (Isa. 40:12); and the psalmist reminds us that all God has to do to feed His creatures is open His hand (Ps. 104:28). "You open Your hand and satisfy the desire of every living thing" (Ps. 145:16, NKJV).

2. He was called "Artaxerxes Longimanus," which is

Latin for "Artaxerxes the long-handed." (The Greek equivalent is "Macrochier.") He may have been called "the long-handed" because his great authority reached out so far, or because he was generous to his subjects. But it was God's hand that moved the king's hand to sign the edict that enabled Ezra to take a remnant of Jews to their land to serve the Lord.

3. Nixon, Richard. *Leaders* (New York: Warner Books, 1982), 1.

4. Hilkiah was high priest during the reign of godly King Josiah and found the Book of the Law while the temple was being repaired (2 Kings 22). Zadok was faithful to King David during David's most trying times, especially when Absalom and Adonijah tried to capture the crown (2 Sam. 15 and 17; 1 Kings 1–2). Phinehas was the courageous priest in Moses' day who was honored for opposing Israel's compromise with the Midianites (Num. 25; Ps. 106:30).

5. Many students believe that Ezra was one of the founders of the synagogue, which in Babylon took the place of the temple as a place for assembly, worship, and teaching.

6. Moses wrote what God told him (Ex. 24:4, 12; Deut. 28:58; 29:21; 30:10; 31:9, 19, 24) and also kept a record of Israel's journeys (Num. 33:2). He left Joshua "the Book of the Law" (Josh. 1:8) to which Joshua added his record (23:6). Samuel wrote in the book (1 Sam. 10:25) and others added to it (1 Chron. 29:29). The Book of the Law apparently was "lost" in the temple, of all places, and recovered during Josiah's day (2 Chron. 34–35). The Jewish scribes were very careful to copy the Scriptures accurately and preserve them from textual corruption. Thanks to their faithfulness and the providence of God, we have the Scriptures today.

7. Zerubbabel didn't have an abundance of Levites in his company, only 733 out of almost 50,000 men, less than 2 percent. One would think that God's special servants would be

anxious to go back to their land and serve, but they decided to stay.

Chapter 4

1. This injunction is also found in Leviticus 11:45; 19:2; 20:7, 26; 21:8; and 1 Peter 1:15-16. When God repeats a command eight times, His people had better pay attention!

2. Christians are exhorted to marry "in the Lord" (1 Cor. 7:39) and not join themselves with unbelievers (2 Cor. 6:14-18). The Old Covenant distinction between Jews and Gentiles no longer applies, for God had made all nations of one blood and there is "no difference" (Acts 10; 17:26; Rom. 3:21-23). The Messiah has come, the work of salvation has been completed, and believing Jews and Gentiles may marry in the Lord and serve God.

3. Three great prayers of confession are found in the Old Testament: Ezra 9, Nehemiah 9, and Daniel 9.

4. When Nehemiah discovered sin, he plucked out the hair of the offenders! (Neh. 13:25)

5. The word "heaviness" (KJV; "self-abasement," NIV) suggests that Ezra fasted during this trying time, not because he was trying to earn God's blessing, but because he was just too burdened to eat.

6. Depending on how you translate the text and determine the various relationships, there were either 110 or 111 offenders.

Chapter 5

1. However, it's difficult to think that God's servants would wait for sixteen years before urging the people to get back to work rebuilding God's house. Did Haggai and Zechariah arrive in Judah much later, sent by God to get the work going again? Or do their books record only the success of their ministry? They may have been urging the people all

along to return to the task for which they had been released from bondage. Ezra doesn't mention them in his book until 5:1. It's likely that God permitted His people to suffer sixteen years of discipline and disappointment to prepare them for the words of His prophets. It's a good illustration of the truth of Matthew 6:33.

2. One of the basic themes of Malachi is the honor of God's name. See my book *Be Amazed* (Victor) for an exposition of Malachi.

3. Morgan, G. Campbell. *The Westminster Pulpit* (London: Pickering and Inglis), vol. 8, 315.

4. Zechariah uses the title "Lord of hosts" thirty-seven times and Malachi twenty-three times. Why should the little Jewish remnant fear the Gentile armies around them when the Lord of Armies is their Savior and Commander? The Hebrew word for "hosts" *[tsaba]* is transliterated as "Sabaoth" in Romans 9:29 and James 5:4. Martin Luther used it in verse 2 of his hymn "A Mighty Fortress Is Our God."

> Did we in our own strength confide,
> our striving would be losing,
> Were not the right man on our side,
> the man of God's own choosing.
>
> Dost ask who that may be? Christ Jesus, it is he;
> Lord Sabaoth his name, from age to age the same,
> And he must win the battle.

Chapter 6

1. In the Authorized Version of Leviticus, words relating to ceremonial cleanliness are used 71 times, and words relating to "uncleanness" 128 times. "Unclean" is used 31 times in Leviticus 11, the chapter that details what the Jews were allowed to eat. Of course, "unclean" refers only to ceremonial defilement and not the condition of the heart. No amount of

washing or sacrificing could of itself make the inner person clean. For inner cleansing, there must be repentance, confession, and faith (Ps. 51).

2. Whatever touched the altar became holy (Ex. 29:37), as well as whatever touched the sanctified vessels of the tabernacle (30:28-29), but the "holiness" of the objects that touched the altar or the vessels couldn't be transmitted to anything else.

3. D. Martyn Lloyd-Jones. *Preaching and Preachers* (London: Hodder and Stoughton, 1971), 24.

Chapter 7

1. Zechariah the postexilic prophet must not be confused with the Zechariah who was martyred in the days of King Joash (2 Chron. 24:20-22) and to whom Jesus referred (Matt. 23:35). Their fathers had the same first name, but this wasn't uncommon in Bible times. Since the Hebrew Bible ends with 2 Chronicles, Jesus was saying, "From the beginning of the Scriptures [Abel's murder in Genesis] to the very end of the Scriptures [Zechariah's murder in 2 Chron.], all the innocent blood that was shed will be held against you." We have no evidence that the Zechariah who ministered with Haggai was ever slain.

2. See chapter 29 of *Born After Midnight*, by A.W. Tozer (Christian Publications, 1959).

3. The Jews certainly knew the terms of God's covenant. If they obeyed, the blessing would overtake them (Deut. 28:2), but if they disobeyed, the curses would catch up with them. "But it shall come to pass, if you do not obey the voice of the Lord your God . . . that all these curses will come upon you and overtake you . . . Moreover all these curses shall come upon you and pursue you and overtake you until you are destroyed" (Deut. 28:15, 45, NKJV).

4. See Revelation 2:5, 16, 21-22; 3:3, 19. Five of the seven

churches to which Jesus wrote were commanded to repent.

5. Students of prophecy aren't agreed as to the starting date for the Captivity. If you begin with 606–605, when the first prisoners were taken to Babylon, then the Captivity ended in 537 when the Jews returned to Judah, led by Zerubbabel and Joshua. If you count from the destruction of Jerusalem and the temple in 586, then the Captivity ended with the dedication of the second temple in 515. If the latter date is what the Lord had in mind, then the completing of the temple was indeed a key event. However, the question in Zechariah 1:12 implies that the seventy years were now over.

6. Jeremiah lamented that nobody had comforted Jerusalem after the city was destroyed (Lam. 1:2, 9, 16-17, 21).

7. The *London Observer,* 2 Jan. 1983. Quoted in *The Columbia Dictionary of Quotations,* compiled by Robert Andrews (New York: Columbia University Press, 1993), 477.

8. The neo-Roman Empire appears again at the end of the age under the control of the Beast (Dan. 7:8; Rev. 13). This empire will be destroyed by the return of Christ in power and great glory (Dan. 2:44-45 and 7:9ff).

9. Alexander's conquests are mentioned in Zechariah 9:1-8, 13.

10. The word "pupil" comes from the Latin *pupilla,* "a tiny doll," referring to the small reflection you see of yourself when you look into another's eyes. The Hebrew word for "apple" (pupil) in Deuteronomy 32:10 is literally "little man."

Chapter 8

1. Kouzes, James M., and Posner, Berry Z. *The Leadership Challenge* (San Francisco: Jossey-Bass Publishers, 1987), xvi.

2. It sunk even lower after the temple was completed. Read the prayer of Ezra (Ezra 9) and the Book of Malachi for proof. When our Lord came to earth, the flame of Jewish

faith was flickering.

3. Unger, Merrill F. *Commentary on Zechariah* (Grand Rapids: Zondervan, 1963), p. 59.

4. In Solomon's temple, the one large candlestick was replaced with ten smaller ones (1 Kings 7:49; 1 Chron. 28:15).

5. Havner, Vance. *The Vance Havner Quote Book,* compiled by Dennis J. Hester (Grand Rapids: Baker Book House, 1986), 111.

Chapter 9

1. The Hebrew word *eretz* can mean either "land" or "earth" depending on the context, and sometimes it isn't easy to determine which is meant. In Zechariah 4:14, *eretz* is obviously "earth," for our God is "lord of the whole earth." The NIV translates *eretz* "land" in 5:3 and 6, meaning the land of Israel; while the KJV and NKJV use "earth," meaning the whole world. I prefer the NIV translation since these visions deal especially with the sins of the Jewish nation against the Law of God.

2. By making a minor change in the Hebrew text, the NIV translators have the white horses going to the west, but the received text has the white horses following the black horses.

3. The KJV translated it "crowns," but how could you put several crowns on one man's head? The Hebrew word is plural, but this refers to the elaborateness of the crown. It was a diadem (Rev. 19:12), one crown with several levels, one on top of the other.

4. The statement "Behold the man" (v. 12) reminds us of what Pilate said to the Jews in John 19:5 when he presented Christ to them. It reminds us of the Gospel of Luke, the Gospel of the Son of Man. "Behold my servant" (Isa. 42:1) reminds us of Mark, the Gospel of the Servant; "Behold

your King" (Zech. 9:9) relates to Matthew, the Gospel of the King; and "Behold your God" (Isa. 40:9) reminds us of the Gospel of John, the Gospel of the Son of God.

5. Some people "spiritualize" these kingdom prophecies and relate them to the church today rather than to a restored Israel in the future. That there are present-day applications of Old Testament passages, no honest student would deny; for the only "Bible" the first-century church had was the Old Testament. But there's a difference between *application* and *interpretation*. Each passage has only one basic interpretation, even though there may be several applications.

Chapter 10

1. However, let's not wait until then to show compassion to the unborn and the elderly. If God's ideal is happy children playing together in the streets and elderly people chatting together, then why not aim for the ideal today? Jesus came that we might have abundant life as well as eternal life, but our modern cities are more and more becoming places of death.

2. For that matter, their fasts didn't accomplish anything because their hearts weren't right with God (Zech. 7:4-14). They only went through a religious ritual that did more harm than good. Better not to do it at all than to do it and not mean it.

3. Contemporary opposition to Jewish evangelism is a subtle new form of anti-Semitism. The Christian church owes so much to Israel, and the best way to pay the debt is to share the Gospel with the Jewish people. If it's wrong to witness to Jews, then Jesus was wrong, and so were Peter and Paul. Jesus wept over Jerusalem and Paul was willing to go to hell for their conversion (Rom. 9:1-3). That ought to be motivation enough for us to lovingly witness to the people who gave us the Bible and the Savior.

Chapter 11

1. The Hebrew word means "to lift up," suggesting that the prophet lifted his voice to proclaim the Word of God. But there's also the idea of a heavy weight that the prophet carries because of the seriousness of the message.

2. The conquest of Philistia had also been predicted by Isaiah (23:1-18), Jeremiah (25:22; 47:4), Ezekiel (26:1-21 and 28:20-24), and Amos (1:9-10).

3. The account of Alexander's visit to the Holy City is recorded by the Jewish historian Josephus in his *Antiquities of the Jews,* book XI.8, sections 3–5.

4. The donkey was the animal used by royalty (2 Sam. 16:2; 18:9; 1 Kings 1:33).

5. Isaiah gave his two sons names that illustrated what he was preaching to the people, and he also dressed scantily, like a prisoner of war, for three years. Jeremiah wore a yoke, publicly broke pottery, and wore a dirty girdle. Ezekiel "played" at war, got a haircut and disposed of the cuttings in three unusual ways, and cut a hole in the wall so he could "escape."

6. Students have a tough time figuring out who these three shepherds were. They scour lists of the names of rulers, priests, and other important people who lived at that time, but we have to confess that we just don't know and it's useless to speculate.

7. History reveals that the Jews have had a tendency to break up into parties and sects rather than try to agree and work together for common goals. Over the centuries, they have produced many different groups, religious and political, and there will be no national unity until the "birth" of the new nation when Messiah comes.

8. In Mark 1:1-3, in the best Greek texts, Mark quotes Malachi 3:1 and Isaiah 40:3 and says, "As it is written in Isaiah the prophet." He names the greater prophet.

Chapter 12

1. The word "Armageddon" is used only in Revelation 16:16. Some students of prophecy prefer "the campaign of Armageddon" since the invasion and attack take place in several stages.

2. That the last great world battle will involve horses and riders is a puzzle to some. But the prophets wrote so that the people could understand, and horses and chariots were the strongest and best equipment an army could have in their day. However, the description of the results of the plague (14:12-15) resembles that of the victims of an atomic blast.

3. The NIV reads "a spirit of grace and supplication," that is, an attitude of heart, and gives "the Spirit" in the margin. But parallel passages suggest that it is the Holy Spirit of God who is referred to (Joel 2:28-29; Ezek. 29:39; and see Peter's reference to Joel's prophecy when the Spirit came at Pentecost (Acts 2:16-21).

4. Having rejected the truth, the Jewish nation fell prey to lies, especially false prophets. Jeremiah had to battle the false prophets in his day, and false prophets will abound in the end times (Matt. 24:4-5, 11, 23-24).

5. Some interpreters apply verse 6 to the Messiah, but the context prohibits this. In verses 2-6, it's clearly the false prophets who are being discussed.

6. The reign of Christ on earth is usually called "the Millennium" because it will last for 1,000 years. "Millennium" comes from the Latin: mille = thousand; annum = year. See Revelation 20:1-7.

7. Some students equate the millennial Jerusalem of Ezekiel 40–48 with the heavenly city described in Revelation 21–22, but to accept that view requires total disregard of several facts. There is no temple in the heavenly city (Rev. 21:22), but Jerusalem in the Kingdom Age will have a temple and a priesthood. Worshipers from all nations will cele-

brate the Jewish Feast of Tabernacles at the kingdom Jerusalem (Zech. 14:16-21), but surely there would be no such worship in the heavenly city. Furthermore, those who don't worship properly will be punished, something we can't begin to imagine happening in the heavenly city. During the Kingdom Age, Jesus will reign in Jerusalem from David's throne (Luke 1:32-33), but the throne in the heavenly city is "the throne of God and of the Lamb" (Rev. 22:3). The heavenly city is "the bride, the Lamb's wife" (Rev. 21:9), while the nucleus of the millennial Jerusalem is the refined Jewish remnant, "the wife of Jehovah" who is now cleansed and restored.

8. Unger, 265–66.

9. Zechariah 14:21 is another evidence that the temple and the priesthood will be important elements of life in the Kingdom Age.

Chapter 13

1. Schlesinger, Arthur M., Jr. "The Decline of Heroes," in *Adventures of the Mind,* edited by Richard Thruelsen and John Kobler (New York: Alfred A. Knopf, 1960), 96.

2. Ibid., 98. In the years that followed the publication of Dr. Schlesinger's essay, especially during the sixties, individualism began to be more acceptable as the younger generation rebelled against "the establishment." With the many options and lifestyles around us, society today may not appear to be very homogeneous, but conformity today is found in the many subcultures that make up society. "There's safety in sameness," says the subculture. "Let's all be different by being alike." So, Dr. Schlesinger's thesis is still true: we're a nation of sheep, and most people are just trying to find their own comfortable fold.

3. Boorstin, Daniel J. *The Image: A Guide to Pseudo-Events in America* (New York: Harper and Row, 1964), 45.